combining the Great Commission and
the Greatest Commandment
in order to raise up...

Disciples Unleashed

Dave Campbell
with Kent Roberts

Copyright © 2016 by Disciples Unleashed, Inc.
All rights reserved, including the right to reproduce this book or portions thereof in any form whatsoever.
Cover designer: Scott Campbell
Manuscript editor: Kelly McGough

≈ ≈ ≈

For more information on Disciples Unleashed, relational discipleship, and other useful tools and information, as well as how *you* can become involved, log on to:

www.disciplesunleashed.com
and
www.reallifeministries.com/missions

All Scripture quotations, unless otherwise indicated, are taken from the *Holy Bible, New International Version, NIV*. Copyright © 1973, 1978, 1984, 2011 by Biblica, Inc. Used by permission.

Other permissions & Copyrights:

Holy Bible, New American Standard Bible, NASB: Scripture taken from the *NEW AMERICAN STANDARD BIBLE®*, Copyright © 1960,1962,1963,1968,1971,1972,1973,1975,1977,1995 by The Lockman Foundation. Used by permission.

Holy Bible, English Standard Version, ESV: copyright © 2001 by Crossway, a publishing ministry of Good News Publishers. Used by permission.

Holy Bible, New Living Translation, NLT: from the Holy Bible, New Living Translation, copyright ©1996, 2004, 2007 by Tyndale House Foundation. Used by permission of Tyndale House Publishers, Inc., Carol Stream, Illinois 60188. All rights reserved.

Dedications:

From Dave Campbell:

I so appreciate the opportunity that our Father has given me to be a part of His work. He, being rich in mercy, has saved me, forgiven me, and now, by His grace, He even allows me to participate in the work of His kingdom (Ephesians 2:4-10).

I dedicate this book to:

Jesus: My King, my Captain, my Lord, my Model and my Savior.

Jim Putman: My Senior Pastor, who lives what he preaches—including the part about "nobody is perfect!" :-) , and who has shown me what Biblical leadership and real relationship look like in the flesh.

Luke Yetter: My Team Leader at Real Life Ministries who has challenged me, coached me, and taught me more in five years than I learned in the first fifty-five.

Janelle Campbell: My beautiful wife, who prayed for me, gently led me toward Christ, loves me, encourages me, and labors with me in His work. I am blessed to walk alongside this woman who taught me kindness, patience, forgiveness, and love, by living them out for me to see.

Kent Roberts: My co-writer who selflessly dove into this project with patience, perseverance and a Kingdom perspective, and who has cared enough to not just write about this, but to become a part of it as well.

From Kent Roberts:

Dave and I took on this project in order to bring glory and honor to God through the writing of this book, and also through those who might read it. Thank you, Lord, for the opportunity to be a part of this whole endeavor.

To my wife and family: Thank you for giving me the time and space to accomplish this goal. Cheryl, you've been more than supportive through this entire wild dream I've had of writing for a living and I appreciate the patience and encouragement you've given me all along the way.

To Dave: Thank you for choosing me to join you on this journey. Digging into the Word and peeling away the layers to reveal Jesus's original plan for discipleship has broadened and deepened my understanding of our Lord and Savior and given me new insights into my own faith journey as well. Thank you for your friendship and for the time to get to know you, both on a relational level, and as a man wholly dedicated to bringing the message and method of Jesus Christ to the entire world, one person at a time.

May this book, in wisdom and application, bless all of those who read it as it did with me in its writing!

Contents

Introduction 9

Chapter 1: Setting Up the Target 13

Chapter 2: To the Ends of the Earth: 25

Chapter 3: Country by Country: 39

Chapter 4: Key Pastors Are Contagious: 55

Chapter 5: Creating the Biblical Model in "Your" Church 69

Chapter 6: Impacting Your Family, Your Friends, and Your Leadership Team 79

Chapter 7: Truly Making a Disciple of Jesus (Who Makes Disciples) ... 89

Chapter 8: It Starts with the "Be" 105

Chapter 9: And, It Works in All Cultures…Even Yours! 119

Chapter 10: Getting Down to the Basics 135

Chapter 11: Where the Rubber Meets the Road 145

Disciples Unleashed

Introduction
What Are You Hoping to Learn Here?

Whether locally, in the United States, or around the world, this is the typical opening question I raise whenever I begin a discussion on Real Life Ministries' Biblically-based discipleship process: *What do you hope to learn by being here today?*

Everyone's answers may vary in scope and range, often enough to fill an entire whiteboard in a manner of minutes, but inevitably these answers center around two central aspirations:

A hope to grow their respective churches.

A desire to reach and connect with more lost people, drawing them to the ultimate, saving grace of our Lord, Jesus Christ.

No matter what everyone says, all have outstanding answers, and all those who voice them have some fantastic goals in mind, without a doubt.

Then I pose this follow-up: *Now, how do you propose we go about doing that?*

Silence!

Oh, that's why you came to the seminar? That's why you picked up this book?

What? You'd like *me* to tell you the answer on how to reach more people, how to connect with the lost, how to effectively and lastingly grow church attendance, or at least tell you the *latest* answer?

You'd like to know the secret of why Real Life Ministries, in Post Falls, Idaho, the tenth most populous city in the thirty-ninth most populous state according to 2014 statistics, has grown from just two couples in 1998 to a congregation of over 8,500 people in less than fifteen short years, some traveling from as far as 50 miles or more on a weekly basis?

You want to learn how we continually get between 85 to 90 percent of our congregation to become involved in small groups? How we took the Biblical model of Jesus and the twelve and applied it as the working discipleship model of RLM? A model so simple, yet so profound, that it was as if God Himself had designed it from the beginning with His church—which we're all called to play a part (Ephesians 4:11-16)—in mind?

Hmm...

How Did We Do It?!

Well...I'm sorry, I can't tell you that.

You see, the problem is that there is no four-step program, no all-encompassing curriculum, no single-page process that I can give you that you can take back to your own town, to your own country, to your own church, only to palm it off on some lower-level lackey and say, "Here, implement this! They say it's supposed to work," adding with a well-worn cynicism and a little smirk, "We'll see."

Wait, wait, wait, though...

Before you put this book down, before you walk out of the next Real Life Ministries (RLM) DiscipleShift seminar, let me say this...

I can't *tell* you about any easy, bullet-point process, but I can *show* you the results.

Even more, I can let a few of the pastors and church leaders from around the world show you the amazing ripple effect of how Jesus's model of discipleship worked for their own once-frustrated flocks, in their own small slice of the world.

You'll meet a shy, soft-spoken pastor from Burundi who now leads a ministry network of over 200 churches spread across six countries in Africa.

You'll be introduced to a pastor from New Zealand who was assigned to a small church with an aging (read: "dying") attendance "in order to put it quietly to bed," in the words of his superiors. How, instead of laying his church peacefully aside, he began to work with his staff and congregation, engaging them in small groups, and sparking an interest in the lives and spiritual growth of one another. The reaction was similar to as if a doctor had applied an electric shock directly to the chest of his little church, bringing new life, new hope, and, most importantly, renewed growth.

You'll meet Pastor Joné and some fellow pastors from Fiji who overcame long-held religious and culturally reinforced walls between clergy and staff, and between men and women, tearing them down to engage with one another on a level of relationship and confidence previously thought taboo and unheard of.

You'll read about some of the volunteers from our own church, Real Life Ministries—some of the most unlikely, unqualified-in-their-own-minds people to ever walk in to a missionary meeting—who now walk alongside pastors from as far and wide as Africa, Southeast Asia, Mexico, India, and the Pacific Islands. This band of committed Christians, walking in the faith of Jesus's intentional relationship model, are building relationships, building trust, and building up these pastors' self-assurance, and their churches, even while facing some of the most vile persecution imaginable.

I can't tell you about any process. But *they* can. They are the ones who can (and will) tell you how disciples of Jesus are being unleashed into today's world.

> *The harvest is great, but the workers are few. So pray to the Lord who is in charge of the harvest; ask him to send more workers into his fields.* — Luke 10:2, NLT

Ultimately, this book is an invitation. An invitation to engage in the method of discipleship first modeled over two thousand years ago by a carpenter's son and twelve of His friends—fishermen, tax collectors, and the most unlikely band of misfits ever gathered. Men who ended up changing the face of religion. Men who ended up changing the world. Led by the Emmanuel. God made flesh. The ultimate example of leader and disciple-maker the world has ever seen.

I can't tell you about any process, but *He* can!
Best of all, He already has.

Disciples Unleashed

Chapter 1
Setting Up the Target: Putting It on *His* Stand, Not Yours

If we can imagine our goal of becoming intentional, relational disciples of Jesus as the bull's-eye of an archery target, then each outer ring of that target should refine our aim, bringing us closer and closer to that ultimate goal: consistently hitting that bull's-eye. So, with that in mind, it stands to reason that our outermost "ring" should be in clarifying a few terms we're going to be using along the way, accurately defining things like "missions," "church," "disciple," and even "Christian." And if we're going to accurately define those terms, it also stands to reason that we should be using God's definitions, found within His Word, yes? For instance...

When We Say "Missions," What Are We Saying?

Well, right away we're going to encounter a bit of a problem.

Do you realize the word "missions" does not appear in the Bible? It's not a Biblical term. And though I believe that it's a Biblical *concept*, as a word, the term "missions" never shows up in Scripture.

We, as Jesus's disciples, are told in the Great Commission to:

> *"...go and make disciples of all nations, baptizing them in the name of the Father and of the Son and of the Holy Spirit, and teaching them to obey everything I have commanded you."* — Matthew 28:19–20, NIV

There is a command there to make disciples "of all nations." In the Christian world, many have named this commission—this command—"missions," and from the onset of the Book of Acts, this is what the apostles and the earliest church did: "go and make disciples." Paul did this. Peter did this. And, as followers of Christ, this commission applies to us today as well.

Missions has always been about making disciples of Jesus who can then make more disciples of Jesus, and on and on. And yet, just as the concept of "church" has in many ways deviated from the Biblical model that Jesus and the apostles gave us, so has "missions" deviated from that same Biblical concept.

The Question behind the Question

Every time I see someone pick up a book on church growth, disciple making, and changing a church culture—including this one—I have to wonder, *What are you hoping to find?*

What is the real pique of your interest?

Is it a numbers game? Could you be trying to find that elusive key to grow your weekly attendance, maybe hoping to fill up a few more empty pews?

Is it seeking out some new avenue of persuasion, something that might convince a few more fence-sitters to cross over the line of faith?

Don't get me wrong—these are not bad ideals at all. They're quite admirable, in fact.

And yet, I want to believe there is more to our curiosity that draws us to the *newest* and *latest*, luring us to some distant city and seating us with a room full of strangers to find some indefinable key to church growth, to spiritual maturity, and disciple making. Over the years, of watching and wondering, of asking and discussing, I've come to believe that maybe there is a little more to the question behind our question.

It's one thing to grow the numbers of weekly church attendance. I mean, who doesn't like to see a full sanctuary? Who doesn't like to hear the lifted voices of a packed congregation singing out praises to our Father?

But what happens when the worship is over, when the message is given, when the stage is empty? What happens when that congregation hits the doors of our church and re-enters the *real world*? How do we keep that spark, that fire, which drew all those people—and all of us as well, for that matter—into our local churches in the first place? After all, the Word of God is not just something to be absorbed into our heads as knowledge, nor is it something to be stored away like a keepsake; it is to be living, active, and transformative in our actual day-to-day lives.

> *But don't just listen to God's word. You must do what it says. Otherwise, you are only fooling yourselves.* — James 1:22, NLT

I believe there is a growing desire within all of us who've made "church" a vital, ongoing practice in our lives to do more than merely attend. Warm bodies in empty seats don't solve the problem of how to bring people into a central, lasting bond with Jesus, active and mature, unleashed into the world to live in relational discipleship with one another, and making more in the process. Those warm bodies have inquisitive hearts, hearts that have been hardened by an overwhelming, suffocating world, and there is a crucial difference between a church leader simply harvesting more lukewarm church attendees and his desire to cultivate active and eager disciples of Jesus.

In fact, it is critical that we begin to develop a church culture of honest and sincere Christ followers, hungry for a deeper, more meaningful relationship with God, with His Son, and with other disciples. This culture should be equipped to become disciples themselves, meeting together in groups, sharing all they have (Acts 2:42–47), and going boldly into a world that desperately needs them, sharing the Gospel and living a life worthy of that good news (Philippians 1:27).

In other words, I firmly believe that any attempt at church growth should be based on the foundational method and message of Jesus Christ Himself.

> *I have brought You glory on earth by finishing the work You gave Me to do... I have revealed You to those You gave Me out of the world...and they have obeyed Your word... For I gave them the words You gave Me and they accepted them.* — John 17:4, 6 & 8, NASB

"We're Hitting Our Target, so What Are We Missing?"

Speaking of going forth boldly, I need to be honest with you for a moment here.

The concept of how we, as Christians, do "church," most particularly here in America, has gotten a bit off target. Not all at once but slowly, over time and generations and, for the most part, in spite of our best intentions. I know that sounds counterintuitive, but hear me out on this.

A lot of churches are firing arrows of messages, methodology, and ideas, and hitting a target of bringing people through the front doors. There are plenty of churches today who feature a dynamic worship service, faithful expository preaching, and all of the necessary components that we feel make up a "good service." And, in these church's minds, they keep hitting their target, doing better and better at this "target" of putting warm bodies in seats.

But is that the right target? Is that Jesus's target?

Jesus was all about bringing people into relationship with Himself, and He was all about compassion for the hurting and mercy for the sinful, but He also pulled no punches when it came to the role, and the cost, of those who chose to follow Him. To use a fishing analogy, most churches today cast a wide net that can potentially "catch" the interest of a good many people, but inevitably the congregation seldom bothers to venture beyond the shallow water of where they were first caught.

What Jesus asks us to do is to abide in Him, and in each other, through intentional connection and relational discipleship. This is what Jesus calls for in Matthew 28 and can be seen through the actions of His disciples in the first chapters of Acts—intentional connection through relational discipleship.

Somewhere along the way we, as a corporate body called "the church," have lost the definition of how to teach one another as Jesus taught—through both compassion *and* intentional relationship. More importantly, we seemed to have forgotten how to *be* disciples and how to *make* disciples as He did it.

These are not things that the pastor needs to preach about once a week to whoever comes through the front doors of a building. These are the things that we, as Christians, are called and compelled to do every day. With everyone. This is *our* Great Commission if we choose to call ourselves followers of Christ.

What's in a Word?

But let's step back for a second and define things by their Biblical definition.

Today, if we look at the word "church," the most common image which comes to people's mind is that of a building—sometimes with a cross on it, sometimes with a pithy saying on its signboard out front. But in the Bible, the concept of church was never about a building, and when the word "church" was used in Scripture (most often ἐκκλησία, or *ekklésia*,[1] in the Greek, see Acts 11:22 & 26 for examples), it was never in reference to a structure with a cross out front and a pithy slogan on a signboard. "Church" was all about the relationships within the body of Christ; the people, gathering together in worship and fellowship, breaking bread and sharing all that they had.

Furthermore, if we say the word "Christian," most people likely think of someone who attends that particular building called "church." Even the people going to the building would say, "Yes, I am a Christian. That's why I'm going to church."

By contrast, in the Bible, the early Christians never had the attitude of "going to church." The concept that Jesus and His apostles taught was all about how the people would *be* the church. These people *were* the church; this concept lies at the heart of what it means to be a "disciple" of Christ—which is yet another confusing and often misused word.

Ask modern-day church attendees if they are a Christian, and most everyone would answer, "Yes, of course."

But, ask these same people if they are a *disciple*, and most would say, "Well, no, I'm just a regular Christian."

---

[1] According to *Strong's Concordance*, the word ekklēsía is derived from two root sources, *ek*, meaning "out from and to," and *kaléō*, meaning "to call." Therefore, ekklēsía are the people, the universal or total body of believers, whom God calls out from the world and into His eternal kingdom.

Taking all three of these terms into account, let's look at the church in Antioch, as described in Acts 11.

> *Now those who had been scattered by the persecution that broke out when Stephen was killed traveled as far as Phoenicia, Cyprus and Antioch, spreading the word only among Jews. Some of them, however, men from Cyprus and Cyrene, went to Antioch and began to speak to Greeks also, telling them the good news about the Lord Jesus. The Lord's hand was with them, and a great number of people believed and turned to the Lord.*
>
> *News of this reached* **the church in Jerusalem, and they** *sent Barnabas to Antioch. When he arrived and saw what the grace of God had done, he was glad and encouraged them all to remain true to the Lord with all their hearts. He was a good man, full of the Holy Spirit and faith, and a great number of people were brought to the Lord.*
>
> *Then Barnabas went to Tarsus to look for Saul, and when he found him, he brought him to Antioch.* **So for a whole year Barnabas and Saul met with the church and taught great numbers of people. The disciples were called Christians first at Antioch.** — Acts 11:19–26, NIV (emphasis mine)

Notice how the term "the church" is used interchangeably with "the people," and that Barnabas and Saul met "with the church," not "in the church."

Also notice that these people were not Christians who became disciples. "The disciples were called Christians first at Antioch," meaning that the people, "the church"—*all* of them—were also, inherently, disciples. I particularly like the way *Strong's Concordance* defines the name "disciple," or in the Greek μαθητής, or mathētḗs, as "a learner; a follower of Christ who learns the doctrines of Scripture and the lifestyle they require; someone with proper instruction from the Bible with its necessary follow-through and life-applications."[2]

Hitting a Target but Missing the Mark... in Church

So in Luke's writings to us in Acts, he is showing us that the church is a gathering together of disciples. It wasn't that the church was full of Christians and a few of them became disciples. On the contrary, you were not considered a Christian *unless* you were a disciple.

I daresay that as the church today, interpreted as the corporate body of Christ, we've gotten off that course. "Church" has become a building that people go to, and if you're committed to the religious doctrine of the church, you might call yourself a "Christian." Furthermore, if you're really, really committed, you might say you are a "disciple."

And this is not simply an American problem. I have seen this over and over in many of the countries we have traveled to over the course of our years of mission work. The reason for this is because we can trace the roots of almost all of those churches across the world to missionaries who came out of a church that had already deviated from the Biblical model given to us by Christ and demonstrated by the first believers in Acts.

This is an inherent problem across the entire religious spectrum of Christianity; congregants all over the world today do church the way they have been shown to do church, whether from Methodist, Baptist, Presbyterian, or Assemblies of God missionaries. Whoever came to do the mission work of a given country—with the purest of heart and the best of intentions—modeled to the indigenous cultures the only thing they knew to teach. Therefore, the Fijians imitated what they had been shown,

---

[2] *Strong's Exhaustive Concordance: New American Standard Bible.* Updated ed. La Habra: Lockman Foundation, 1995. http://www.biblestudytools.com/concordances/strongs-exhaustive-concordance/

as did the Africans, the Southeast Asians, the Central Americans, Australians, New Zealanders, and many others.

I remember, for example, when a team of us traveled to Fiji. We met with a pastor and shared the concepts of relational discipleship with him. He was a pastor in the Assembly of God (AoG) denomination and in fact was the western district superintendent over more than 100 churches throughout the area. The church we attended was one of the largest AoG churches in the surrounding community, with more than 1,000 members attending several weekend services. Our team was invited to share our message of relational discipleship as a part of that particular weekend's service.

As we arrived, we began talking with people, greeting them, shaking hands, and generally getting a feel for the community and the congregation. Soon, an elder came out and escorted us to the pastor's office. There, we sat with the pastor, antsy to get underway. Instead, we were told simply to wait and the elder would return at the appropriate time. When the elder returned, we were escorted down the center aisle, along with the pastor, through the entire congregation, who were now all seated by this time. Not a word was spoken. The pastor gave his message, and then we were given the chance to give ours. Afterward, we were again escorted silently down the center aisle, into the pastor's office, and the door was closed.

Only then was the congregation dismissed. Little did we know that the few minutes before service, until we were escorted away, and then our brief time at the pulpit delivering our message, would be the *only* time we would get to relate to the congregation…at all.

Why was the church service performed in this way?

Because that was what had been shown them. That was the only way the pastor and his staff had known how to "do church."

...*and* in Missions

The fundamental that I feel we need to return to, as a church and as missionaries, is to get back to *His* Biblical model of relational discipleship.

Somewhere along the line, this thread of making disciples as a reproducible model was lost, and the more social and charitable aspects of mission work came to the fore. And, just like with the direction today's church has taken, this aspect of mission work is not necessarily wrong, unless it risks supplanting disciple-making as the primary reason for *doing* missions.

Providing healthcare, building homes, digging wells, and feeding the hungry are all honorable and noble pursuits, and should be a vital part of Christian ministry and missionary work. We can see through the examples of Acts 2, Acts 4, and others that the gathering together of believers as "the church" involved a good deal of compassion and selflessness:

> *All the believers were one in heart and mind. No one claimed that any of their possessions was their own, but they shared everything they had.* — Acts 4:32, NIV

Yet, clearly, Jesus's desire for all who claim to be His followers is to live out His command and commission, and in which He leaves little room for doubt that His top priority is not only love but intentional, relational discipleship.

Changing Our Aim

I know this idea of changing our aim to the real target of Jesus's model of relational discipleship may ruffle a few feathers. And again, let me re-emphasize, there is nothing inherently wrong with the mindset of many of the fine international missionary groups who provide for people's well-being around the world. These organizations are doing a great job at what they do; the heart behind many of these agencies' services is to have compassion and love for people, and to show them Jesus through their actions and intentions.

But I *will* say that even these noble goals cannot be the sole target of our involvement in the lives of these people and cultures if we intend to call ourselves true followers of Jesus. His teachings, His ministry, and His example of relational discipleship need to be at the forefront of our minds if we intend to call ourselves disciples who make disciples, and to come alongside pastors from around the world in order to do that.

So who *should* be meeting the needs and loving on these people from all over the world?

The answer, as you would expect, is that it should be God's people—the church. After all, this is what the body of Christ does—if there is someone hungry, we should feed them; if people are hurting, we should find a way to help them; and if people need [insert your own heart of compassion], we should be the hands and feet of Jesus throughout the world.

Our concept in missions at Real Life Ministries, what we feel is our role, is that we need to help churches first and foremost become disciple-making churches. As those churches become disciplined and productive disciples of Jesus, the natural byproduct will be that they will grow in influence and "fruit," reaching out into their community as the hands and heart of Jesus Christ.

I believe the Biblical model Jesus gave us is this: Be real disciples of Jesus who make more disciples of Jesus in a caring, relational, and reproducible model—in your town, in your region, in your country, and even all around the world. Then, as these disciples of Jesus multiply, groups of disciples (as the church) grow to become His hands and feet to bless and minister to those within their own indigenous community.

This can be the difference between making disciples and making dependents. We are not called to make "converts"; we are called to make disciples. The church (the body of believers) raised from within the communities they serve are the ones designed to do it much more efficiently than any missions organization could ever hope to do it. And it all starts with those of us called to "missions" changing our aim and striving to hit the right target—Jesus's target!

But just who *is* called to missions?

The answer is every believer. Every disciple of Jesus. Every Christian. Everyone who claims His name.

And where is your "mission field"? For all of us, it is wherever we are—our homes, our neighborhoods, our communities. It is also wherever God leads—whether in our own community, to another city, another country, or around the world.

> *"...you will receive power when the Holy Spirit has come upon you; and you shall be My witnesses both in Jerusalem, and in all Judea and Samaria, and even to the remotest part of the earth."* — Acts 1:8, NASB

That is the focus of this book you now hold. Together, let's see if we can't zero in on how to find our best aim, hitting the target of making disciples through intentional relationship with one another. Along the way, we'll use both Biblical and real-life (as opposed to Real Life Ministries) examples of what it means to live out this calling, by people who have done it well, and people who have done it poorly but had someone walking with them to help them back up.

You know...as disciples do.

So, let's go meet some people living out the intentionality of Jesus Christ and inviting others to live it out along with them. And, along the way, let's meet Him as well...

Bible verses to consider

Matthew 28:18-20	Matthew 4:19
James 1:22	Luke 6:40
John 17:4-8	Acts 2:42-47
Acts 11:19-26	Acts 1:8

Study questions for further discussion
(Whether in your personal study, or within a small group setting.)

*Discuss the Biblical definitions and the personal applications of:

Disciple;

Church;

Christian;

and, Missions.

*How would having specific definitions and a more grounded understanding of the Biblical focus of terms such as church, disciple, and Christian, help you know what "target" Jesus intends you to shoot for?

Chapter 2
To the Ends of the Earth: a Worldwide Movement

...and there was an Ethiopian eunuch, a court official of Candace, queen of the Ethiopians, who was in charge of all her treasure; and he had come to Jerusalem to worship, and he was returning and sitting in his chariot, and was reading the prophet Isaiah. Then the Spirit said to Philip, "Go up and join this chariot." Philip ran up and heard him reading Isaiah the prophet, and said, "Do you understand what you are reading?" And he said, "Well, how could I, unless someone guides me?" And he invited Philip to come up and sit with him. Now the passage of Scripture which he was reading was this:

> *"He was led as a sheep to slaughter;*
> *And as a lamb before its shearer is silent,*
> *So He does not open His mouth.*
>
> *"In humiliation His judgment was taken away;*
> *Who will relate His generation?*
> *For His life is removed from the earth."*

The eunuch answered Philip and said, "Please tell me, of whom does the prophet say this? Of himself or of someone else?" Then Philip opened his mouth, and beginning from this Scripture he preached Jesus to him. As they went along the road they came to some water; and the eunuch said, "Look! Water! What prevents me from being baptized?" And Philip said, "If you believe with all your heart, you may." And he answered and said, "I believe that

Jesus Christ is the Son of God." And he ordered the chariot to stop; and they both went down into the water, Philip as well as the eunuch, and he baptized him. When they came up out of the water, the Spirit of the Lord snatched Philip away; and the eunuch no longer saw him, but went on his way rejoicing. – Acts 8:26–39, NLT

The Influence of a Chance Encounter

If you're ever fortunate enough to travel to the small African country of Ethiopia and then visit any corner of a Christian community there, you'll no doubt find that people hold up this small story of Philip and the Ethiopian eunuch very proudly and very dearly. Not out of a sense of undue self-importance as in, "Hey, look at us—we're mentioned in Scripture!" but more in a sense of solidarity, of rejoicing and celebration.

Ethiopia is considered the gateway to the presence of Jesus Christ throughout the continent—a key Christian influence all through recorded history. This story in the book of Acts is why. The indigenous people there consider themselves the "light of Africa" because of this singular person having the Gospel told to him by a disciple of Jesus, and then going "on his way rejoicing" all the way back to his homeland, where he spread the message of Jesus Christ's saving grace throughout the nation.

Even before this time, there has been an historical Semitic thread that runs through the oral traditions of Ethiopia. King Haile Selassie claimed the royal ancestry of all of the kings of Ethiopia could be traced back to the marriage between King Solomon and the Queen of Sheba. There is an interesting quotation in the *International Standard Bible Encyclopedia* that reads:

> The Sabean inscriptions found in Abyssinia go back some 2,600 years and give a new value to the Bible references as well as to the constant claim of (Roman-Jewish scholar)

Josephus that the queen of Sheba (Saba), was a "Queen of Ethiopia."[3]

Even beyond the historical traditions, I think it's interesting to note that this Biblical account points up two very specific facts about this man who "had come to Jerusalem to worship." First, that he was not a member of the people of Israel, God's chosen people. In that time and culture he would have been considered a pagan, a gentile. Yet, somehow, he was drawn to the epicenter of Jewish worship to join with them, bowing in reverence to their God, in their country, in their city.

The trip alone would have involved several weeks' travel for the man, and likely an entourage as well. This would not have been an inexpensive proposition. If, following in Jewish ritual (and there is no reason to think the man would not), his intended worship would have involved a certain knowledge of prayer and sacrifice, this would mean a likely history of Jewish religiosity within his family, or possibly within the palace. Maybe even through the queen herself. And yet, could he have known that as a gentile he would only be allowed into the outer courts of the temple?

Even more, his ethnic standing was complicated by the second fact written within the Scripture: He was also a eunuch. As such, his presence in the temple would most certainly have been strictly forbidden, as is written in Deuteronomy 23:1: "No one who is emasculated or has his male organ cut off shall enter the assembly of the Lord."

If he had not known this—given that he makes the journey, it seems likely he did not—these laws and prohibitions certainly could have perplexed and frustrated him. Yet, as is written, his curiosity would not be abated. Could it be that some high-ranking Jewish official extended grace to him? Could a rabbi, a Pharisee even, have given him a copy of the book of Isaiah to study on his return home? Or could he have used some of the money from the queen's coffers and purchased the

---

[3] This quote and facts on the intertwined history of Ethiopia, the Gospel, and the people of Israel thanks to research from the Global Christian Center. http://globalchristiancenter.com/christian-living/lesser-known-bible-people/31308-the-eunuch-of-ethiopia

Scripture? Isaiah is one of the larger tomes of the Jewish Bible. At the time, such a scroll would have taken over a year for a learned scribe to write, and as such would have been quite valuable. And though we truly don't know how it came to be in his possession, this very scroll was the one the man was reading aloud as Philip approached his caravan.

One Man Can Make a Difference

> *"This man (Simeon Bachos the Eunuch) was also sent into the regions of Ethiopia, to preach what he had himself believed, that there was one God preached by the prophets, but that the Son of this (God) had already made (His) appearance in human flesh, and had been led as a sheep to the slaughter; and all the other statements which the prophets made regarding Him."* — St. Irenaeus of Lyons, in his book *Adversus haereses (Against the Heresies)*, written in 180 A.D.

There has been much speculation within the Ethiopian churches on this mysterious eunuch's identity. And yet, through this auspicious representation in Christian Scripture, the modern-day Ethiopian believers have been able to resist a good many intentional attacks on their religion and influence, primarily from Islamic communities through the Muslim permeation into the national government and the pouring of money into the more populated areas in order to build mosques. The light of Christianity in Africa remains steadfast and strong because of the Ethiopian official from Queen Candace's court coming back after his possibly frustrating journey to Jerusalem, after the message of a life-altering scroll, and after the God-ordained encounter with Philip along the road from Jerusalem to Gaza. His influence remains throughout the country, even to today.

Brendan Pringle wrote on this in his excellent article, "Ethiopia: The First Christian Nation?":

The Acts of the Apostles describe the baptism of an Ethiopian eunuch shortly after the death of Christ. Eusebius of Caesaria, the first church historian, in his "Ecclesiastical History," further tells of how the eunuch returned to diffuse the Christian teachings in his native land shortly after the Resurrection and prior to the arrival of the Apostle Matthew...

Before the Ethiopian king Ezana (whose kingdom was then called Aksum) embraced Christianity for himself and decreed it for his kingdom (c. 330 A.D.), his nation had already constituted a large number of Christians.

As the authors of "Abyssinian Christianity" conclude, "the promotion of the new faith developed into the single point of personal and public identification and unity for Abyssinians." Christianity became the centralizing force behind the Ethiopian empire, which endured through 1974, despite religious and political threats from all sides.

As we see with Abyssinia, and Israel before it, a nation isn't confined to political boundaries. Rather, it is defined by a group of people who share a common heritage. For the Ethiopians, this shared heritage was Christianity. [4]

The Next Ring of Our Target: to the Ends of the Earth—Entire Countries and Cultures *Can* Be Influenced

God is moving all over the world to call believers back to His one and only plan—be disciples of Jesus who make more disciples. There's no arguing that the Apostle Paul was able to

---

[4] "Ethiopia: The First Christian Nation?" article published by Brendan Pringle, *International Business Times*, March 2014. http://www.ibtimes.com/ethiopia-first-christian-nation-1110400

make disciples who could make more disciples on his missionary journeys throughout Asia and the Mediterranean, among the most notable being a young man named Timothy.

> *The things which you have heard from me in the presence of many witnesses, entrust these to faithful men who will be able to teach others also.* — 2 Timothy 2:2, NASB

These disciples, in turn, boldly preached the Gospel wherever they lived, and their impact still resonates today through cities, regions, and countries over the entire world.

Philip changed the course of the Ethiopian eunuch's life. And, when the queen's treasurer returned to his homeland, the man spread the Gospel far and wide, all across his country and beyond.

Even today can we see the influence of one man and the impact he can have in moving with the power of the Holy Spirit throughout an entire nation and beyond, and this brings us to the next ring of our target for Jesus's model of relational discipleship: the willingness to see and become a part of God's worldwide movement to call believers back to His one and only plan.

As Brendan Pringle writes: "A nation is not always confined to political boundaries." Nor is it always confined by geographical proximity. Take the diverse island nation of Fiji, a country comprised of over 300-plus islands, 500-plus islets, and over 7,100 square miles, located 1,100 nautical miles off the New Zealand coast in the heart of the Pacific.

In Fiji, we have been blessed to partner with a man whose influence has acted as a catalyst in igniting an entire region, rippling throughout the world, with the saving grace of Jesus Christ. This man has made it his mission among the island nation to spread the Gospel to as many communities there as he can reach, and his name is Joné Kata.

Joné is a pastor, Bible school director, and missionary, with a great heart and passion for sharing the Gospel of Jesus. Through his connection with RLM, and while Joné was visiting the states on a speaking tour, he came to our church here in Post Falls and went through the DiscipleShift process (at that time called Immersion). He was so impressed with the simplicity of Jesus's model of relational disciple making that he asked if someone could come to Fiji and share this message of Immersion with a gathering of key pastors in the island nation.

It took some doing, but a few years later, we were able to coordinate the trip. To our surprise, there honestly wasn't a ton of response at first.

Oh, it was all good, all well received, but we could tell there was a bit of confusion and hesitation among the gathered pastors and their staff. Over the following months, and during conversations Joné had with friends and coaches here at RLM, we realized that not much had taken root during our time there, and there was really very little ongoing fruit.

For his part, Joné in his heart was just as frustrated as we were. Like the Ethiopian official who had a burning personal desire to follow God and spread the good news of the Gospel, Joné wanted to see the Biblical model of making disciples who can then make disciples enter into his country.

There are many distinct cultural layers within the Fijian communities, but the two primary ethnicities are the native Fijians (those of Melanesian or Polynesian ancestry and indigenous to the islands) and Indo-Fijian (those of Indian ancestry brought to the islands as indentured laborers in the late 1800s and early 1900s).

Joné Kata is one of the few individuals who holds enough influence to be able to bridge the gap between each of these distinct, proud lineages. Almost never do you see a deep, personal interaction between the two cultures, but with Joné acting as an encouraging mediator, he is able to build and maintain significant, long-term contacts within both. In addition, he has opened up avenues of communication with several other key island countries in the region, including Papua New Guinea, Vanuatu, and others.

Despite the initial difficulties, and the long-term process of bridging cultural gaps, Joné remained convinced that Jesus's model of relational discipleship was a vital next step toward spreading the Gospel among the Fijian communities. He began to turn his Gospel message from one of evangelism to an all-encompassing championing of the discipleship process. He wouldn't let it die, and he was persistent enough that a few years later, through his ongoing connections here at RLM, he convinced us to return.

When we did, we found a huge response this time, and Joné was the catalyst. Behind the scenes, he had been working tirelessly, laying the groundwork in making a network of connections throughout the islands, even raising up a key team from within his own family and within his church that were supporting him in his efforts. He continued to tell everyone he met about this Biblical process of discipleship. Even more, Joné had pastors preparing materials and questions for our DiscipleShift experience.

Through Joné's tireless work ethic, this time our trip bore substantial fruit—building on the seeds that had been planted with the first trip. Jesus's model was embraced with enthusiasm by a good many of the pastors present and, almost at once, fruit began to grow on the vine.

One major incident of success is worth noting.

One of our coaches was leading a team from a Fijian church in an icebreaker game we call "Have You Ever." We do this game at the outset of our sessions to gauge how well teams work together, what lines of communications are open, and where we might provide a little more help in establishing relationships in the manner that Jesus asks of us within our close Christian circles.

It was clear from the outset that the group was a little hesitant to interact, somewhat with each other, but most evidently with their senior pastor. This, actually, was something we expected.

Churchgoers, both congregants and staff, hold their senior pastor in high reverence, almost as if placing him on a pedestal. We have found this to be so throughout the world, but even more pronounced within countries of tribal cultures and tribal heritage where we've visited. Sadly, this hierarchical model is one the Fijian churches captured from Western culture, as missionaries first began working among the island nation.

It is not uncommon for Fijian pastors to not even talk to a church member prior to their sermon. In fact, many times all members must be seated before the pastor is escorted down the center aisle. Then, as the sermon concludes, he is escorted back out, again without a word. If you desire to have an audience with him, you must go through several layers of his staff and then maybe, only maybe, will you get an audience with the revered man himself.

While the Fijian group played "Have You Ever," several of the members worked well together, laughing and joking, ribbing each other and playfully pushing and jockeying for position. However, no one dared approach the pastor. He played the game by the rules, but with an obvious separateness due to his status and position.

During one of the later sessions, we pulled the pastor aside and asked him, "Would you be willing to participate more openly during our discussions? Would you be willing to open yourself up a little more, to be a little more transparent? Maybe take part in one of the games, and have a little fun, and joke like others of your staff?"

To our surprise, the pastor's eyes widened and his face broke into a sly grin. "You mean...I can?"

"Absolutely," I encouraged him. "What do you think your staff would do?"

The man's grin widened. "Let's find out."

During the next round, the pastor stepped in to participate. Immediately his staff stepped back, allowing the man full rein to accomplish the objective. Undeterred, the pastor began to rib some of his staff, even good-naturedly pushing a couple of them to rile them up.

It worked. The game continued for several more rounds, and the environment changed dramatically. The group began to treat the pastor as just another member of the staff.

That afternoon, during some deep, personal testimonials and discussion, the pastor spoke up with some of his own heartfelt admissions, and the group responded in kind. It turned out to be one of the best sessions of the entire weekend. Walls had been demolished, cultural and ordered boundaries had been crossed, and the entire group was the better for it.

This is a key component of discipleship that we fully encourage—openness, transparency, and a willingness to "go deep." Of course, as I said in the previous chapter, there are layers to any successful relationship. It would be foolhardy for a pastor to stand at the podium and expose his deepest, darkest struggles and weaknesses. Yet, there is a certain level of honesty that can, and should, be attained between a pastor and congregation; another layer with his staff; and finally, a deeper layer of vulnerability with trusted friends and family.

This too is something Jesus models for us in Scripture. There was constantly a crowd around the Messiah, and He loved them and spoke openly with them. Within the crowd, Jesus also had his twelve apostles, those who He broke bread with and shared fellowship. Then, within the twelve, there were Peter, John, and James, the ones He held in special favor, His key, core leaders, and the ones who witnessed His transfiguration and were specifically invited by Him to hear and see more than any of His other followers.

Those who follow the relational discipleship model of Christ continually break down social, political, religious, and cultural walls. These barriers need to crumble, as they are the ones that hold people back from establishing true, lasting relationships of the kind Jesus made with His diverse group of twelve.

Only through breaking down those walls are we able to fully enjoy the process of growing together in Christ and growing closer with each other. Only then can we take pleasure in the resulting joy that God longs to give us. A joy that will surely weave its way through the church body and even into the lives of the pastoral staff, because we will choose to develop real, deep and intimate friendships with trusted people with whom we can be open and transparent.

A Pastor of Pastors

How do we know Joné Kata "gets it"?

Our staff works closely not only with Joné, but with several of his closest staff, and a number of other pastors in churches around the region. We get to see Joné working and living out this relational discipleship within his family, his leadership team, and his sphere of influence around the Fijian nation, because we are also in communication with many of them.

The model that these pastors and churches have embraced has had a huge impact and a ripple effect throughout the islands, spreading to other island nations and even as far as Australia, all led by one man with a vision to see things differently, beyond culture, beyond tradition, and beyond boundaries of politics and geography.

To paraphrase Brendan Pringle, as with the Ethiopian eunuch in his homeland, and as with Israel before it, the Fijian nation isn't confined to political boundaries. Rather, it is defined by a group of people who share a common cause—the shared heritage of Christianity, and the desire of Jesus Christ to live in relational discipleship with one another. This is what the embers of a global awakening look like—an awakening to the Biblical model of discipleship that goes far beyond any one church, one man, or one experience, but to which we can all attest to.

> *I brought glory to you here on earth by completing the work you gave me to do... I have revealed you to the ones you gave me from this world. They were always yours. You gave them to me, and they have kept your word. Now they know that everything I have is a gift from you, for I have passed on to them the message you gave me. They accepted it and know that I came from you, and they believe you sent me...During my time here, I protected them by the power of the name you gave me. I guarded them so that not one was lost...I am praying not only for these disciples but also for all who will ever believe in me through their message. I pray that they will all be one, just as you and I are one— as you are in me, Father, and I am in you. And may they be in us so that the world will believe you sent me.* — John 17:4–6, 8, 12, 20–21, NLT

This is God's plan. And, if it is God ordained, it will work, and in fact, it is working. There is no plan B, because there has never been a need for one.

Over the course of history, churches have tried to make a plan B, ignoring or misusing Jesus's methods, and honoring only His message. But both His message (of seeking and saving the lost; of going and making disciples) and His methods (servant leadership; relational discipleship through authentic transparency) are vital.

As I said, there is no better plan, no plan B, because none is needed.

All we truly need is to follow Jesus and His model—message and method combined—and lives will be changed. And not only that, churches will be transformed, cultures will shift, countries will be impacted, and our world will be changed.

Jesus came to seek and save the lost (Luke 19:10). To this day, and until the day He returns, He is still going about His Father's business, using His Church and His followers to make His disciples in relational environments as He has modeled for us, and wishes for us to model for each other.

"I pray that they will all be one, just as you and I are one..."

"Very truly I tell you, whoever believes in me will do the works I have been doing, and they will do even greater things than these..."

To the Ends of the Earth: a Worldwide Movement

Bible verses to consider

Acts 8:26-39   Revelation 5:8-10

John 17:4-21   John 3:16-17

Luke 19:10   Matthew 24:14

Study questions for further discussion

*How can God use one person to impact the world?

*What would it take for *you* to become that one person?

*What is God's plan, according to His word, to impact the whole world for Jesus?

Chapter 3
Country by Country: He Is Working His Plan

...the eleven disciples proceeded to Galilee, to the mountain which Jesus had designated. When they saw Him, they worshiped Him; but some were doubtful. And Jesus came up and spoke to them, saying, "All authority has been given to Me in heaven and on earth. Go therefore and make disciples of all the nations, baptizing them in the name of the Father and the Son and the Holy Spirit, teaching them to observe all that I commanded you; and lo, I am with you always, even to the end of the age." — Matthew 28:16–20, NASB

There is very little doubt that this piece of Scripture, what Christians call "the Great Commission," is one of the primary foundations of a Jesus follower's spiritual walk. Jesus told His disciples, and through them told all of us who believe in His name, to "go therefore and make disciples." I like how Eugene H. Peterson's *The Message* paraphrases verse 19:

"Go out and train everyone you meet, far and near, in this way of life..."

Being a disciple of Christ truly is a way of life. The world around us truly is a training ground for being a light to this broken world, for walking in that light, and for drawing others into the light. The Messiah modeled this way of life, within this training ground, on a daily basis with His chosen twelve, and even more directly in relationship with His inner circle of three, Peter, John, and James.

Discipleship is often described as a connection or bond between a teacher and a student. Jesus was known throughout Jerusalem and the surrounding area as a charismatic and knowledgeable rabbi. Having a known rabbi extend an invitation to learn under his tutelage would have been considered quite an honor, especially to a host of such unlikely candidates as the fishermen, tent makers, tax collectors, and others who the Messiah called out to follow Him. Yet what Jesus was inviting these followers into was much more than a summons to learn as students. He invited them into a relationship.

> *Now you are my friends, since I have told you everything the Father told me. You didn't choose me. I chose you. I appointed you to go and produce lasting fruit...* — John 15:15–16, NLT

The Third Ring of Our Target: Nations Are Being Impacted

As we'll learn throughout this book, the most effective method of discipleship, the method Jesus modeled with His own disciples, is one built within the intentionality of a committed relationship. This is no mere friendly connection, but a lasting bond built on transparency and trust—one grounded in truth and devoted to the nurturing and growth of those within that relationship.

By studying the way Jesus made disciples and applying those principles in today's church, we too can become effective disciple makers, called by Jesus and ordained by God to spread the Gospel to the ends of the earth.

By being both a true follower and an intentional leader.

By creating and nurturing real relationships.

By making disciples who then make more disciples through a process that is easily reproducible, and by being aligned and unified as a church.

The first ring of our target is that we must know and follow God's definitions, not our own. We must also follow God's model, not our own.

The next ring is that God is moving powerfully to impact the world by calling His true followers back to this model, Jesus's model. It is happening right now, and it is powerful! The ring we're talking about now is that, nation by nation, whole countries are seeing tremendous fruit because real people are courageously choosing to follow Jesus's model, His methods, and His message.

In fact, let me tell you a story illustrating just one example of what I mean.

There is a man I have been blessed to get to know over the past few years. He has grown to be the embodiment of what discipleship looks like within the day-to-day life of a man and pastor who we've loved and admired over the years here at Real Life Ministries.

His name is Peter Barinzigo, or simply Pastor Peter, from the African country of Burundi.

Pastor Peter

Like many children growing up in the impoverished communities of Africa, neither of Peter's parents were born or raised within the influence of a Christian community, though now, Peter is proud to say his mother has begun putting Jesus first in her life.

When Peter was thirteen years old, he became interested in the church gatherings held not far from his small community. He often traveled by himself to where these meetings were held, listening in rapt attention for hours on end. Every time, he would look on as people stepped forward, sometimes a few, sometimes dozens, to accept the invitation to turn their lives over to Christ. And soon, he too accepted the invitation of Jesus as Lord and Savior, and was baptized.

But after finishing school, he was torn between his budding faith in Christ and the allure of the world unfolding before him. Even within the poverty of his Burundi village, the dust-strewn streets and one-room shacks, Peter was trying to live and experience the fullest of life through the flesh and the Spirit. It was soon clear to him that finding any sense of satisfaction and pleasure was like chasing after the wind, or as the teacher says in Ecclesiastes, "meaningless under the sun."

After two years of being torn by his two worlds, Peter turned his focus solely on Christ, becoming leader of the choir at his local village church and doing some ministry duties as well.

These small duties have since flourished into a full-time pastorship of over seventeen years. He has a beautiful, loving wife who leads a women's ministry at his church, and his first born—of five children—is a teacher of Sunday school there.

"We are helping many people in many ways, according to our capacity," he has said. "Our churches focus on preaching and making disciples, though one of the particular challenges is that we try to provide what best we can for over 200 children who are orphans. Burundi is very poor, and HIV is a major concern in our region. There are many widows as well. Some children can only find one meal every few days. We try to relocate them to their families, or others, but they too are very poor."

I've seen what he speaks of firsthand. Burundi is indeed a tough area in which to live.

There are constant threats of natural disasters, including regional earthquakes and heavy rains in the winter through early spring, which cause flooding and wash away entire mud-and-brick-made villages, followed by months of scorching summer heat, bringing on drought and famine for those same displaced villagers.

Civil war remains a devastating issue. According to a recent profile by Peace Direct, "the conflicts, rooted in political and historical tensions between the ethnic Hutu majority and Tutsi minority populations, have killed more than 300,000 people (over the last forty years, in a nation with a total population relatively the size of New York City). Although much of the violence has subsided in recent years, political instability and unresolved grievances continue to threaten inter-ethnic cooperation and security in the country." [5]

And, of course, there's the poverty. When I was there, Peter's car (a rare possession in the country) could barely make it up the hill on the little dirt road to his house.

---

5 "Burundi: Conflict Profile, Insight on Conflict" article published by Peace Direct, April 2015.
http://www.insightonconflict.org/conflicts/burundi/conflict-profile/

First Impressions and Changed Lives

I first met Peter and another fellow pastor from Burundi, Pastor Frederick, through a very mission-passionate woman who attends our church here at RLM. She had recently gone on a mission to Africa, where she'd met these two pastors, each one zealous for the Lord and eager to undertake the next God-led step of their ministries.

It was because of their interest that she felt God placing it on her heart to bring them together with us. Her desire was that we could help share the focus and intent of Jesus's model of discipleship with them, training and equipping them to take this model, His model, back to their own respective churches and villages.

At the time though, it was not a financial feasibility for our team to make a trip focused solely on the region of Burundi. However, we were getting ready to send a missions team to visit a long-established RLM missions team in Ethiopia, and within the next few months, we were able to set up financing to fly Peter and Frederick there to join us on a discipleship-equipping trip for African pastors.

When Peter and Frederick arrived, they spent the next twelve days traveling to different area cities with our team, ministering, sharing rooms, meals, and fellowship, and hearing us speak to people, over and over again, about Jesus's discipleship process.

Pastor Frederick made an immediate impact on our team. He is a big guy with a big, booming, radio-announcer kind of voice. Boisterous and jovial, Frederick always seemed willing to stand with us during our seminars, sharing his testimony and encouraging the other pastors we met along the way.

Needless to say, we held high hopes for Frederick.

Pastor Peter, on the other hand, is a very quiet man. Compared with Frederick, Peter is more reserved and almost shy; his English is not all that strong, and yet being only one of seven languages he speaks, he actually manages quite well. Still, given even this slight communication difference, I wasn't sure how much of what we were sharing was soaking in.

Toward the end of our time together, while we were in Sodo and after spending a little time shopping, we were sharing yet another meal together at the culmination of a long day's worth of seminars. We were all winding down our time with each other, debriefing and decompressing. Those of us from RLM remained impressed with the enthusiasm and eagerness of Pastor Frederick. But with only a day or two remaining in our journey, we still hadn't unraveled how much of what we shared along the way had been impactful to Pastor Peter, let alone his thoughts on the whole process. I was reflecting on these questions when I noticed Pastor Peter had disappeared.

This was worrisome. Peter had never before missed any of our meals together, and now we couldn't find him at all. Not to mention that where we were staying was in a guesthouse surrounded by vast grasslands and miles of endless jungle. And nightfall was fast approaching.

Like I said, it was worrisome.

I excused myself and decided to have a look around.

Finally I found him, quite a ways from our guesthouse actually, walking by himself, his head down, his eyes focused in concentration, his mouth in a grimace and his head occasionally shaking from side to side.

As I approached him, I could tell that not only were his eyes focused, but he was crying. My first thoughts were, *This poor guy. He's been with us for two weeks now. He's lonely. He doesn't comfortably speak the language. He doesn't have anyone that he's close to along with him. He's probably exhausted and come to the end of his rope.*

I came up, put my arm around him, and asked, "Peter, are you okay?"

Through the tears, he turned to me and said something I will never forget. "This has been the best two weeks of my life. I have learned so much about how I could pastor better, and Jesus's model of discipleship. I'm so excited to get home. I see now how He wants me to lead my church when I return to Burundi."

The Great Commission and the Greatest Commandment, Played Out in Real Time

Much to our surprise and joy, our time together had been the "best two weeks" of Peter's life. Naturally, and due in no small fact to this revelation by our friend, the time there had a huge impact on me and the rest of our team as well. We returned to the states energized and with a renewed sense of focus, staying in touch with both Frederick and Peter.

Frederick has remained focused on a ministry which addresses many of the economic and social issues facing his country and his people. He was a willing participant while we were there, and his heart even to this day remains steadfast for the mission of the Lord in his region.

Perhaps Frederick was looking for the same thing that the American churches had been bringing to the region for decades prior to our arrival. Through no fault of his own, Frederick was looking for us to come as so many had done before—spreading our Gospel message, evangelizing, baptizing, building a few churches, orphanages, or medical centers, perhaps monetarily helping his ministry, and then moving on. After all, this had been the model of American missionary work for decades within their culture and country, so why would he see us any differently?

But Pastor Peter had been impacted on a clearly personal, life-changing level.

Therefore if anyone is in Christ, he is a new creature; the old things passed away; behold, new things have come. — 2 Corinthians 5:17, NASB

Very truly I tell you, whoever believes in me will do the works I have been doing, and they will do even greater things than these, because I am going to the Father. — John 14:12, NIV

Then there was the issue of being real, open, and transparent, a vital key in the honest development of the discipleship process.

One of the deepest, most entrenched cultural (and, in many ways, human nature) chasms we've encountered, one all too common in many impoverished communities, is that of the lens of awe and reverence through which these local churchgoers and villagers choose to see their leadership—be they village elders, elected officials, or religious leaders. There can be no fault. There can be no weakness. And therefore, unfortunately, there can be no transparency.

The tension of bias and reverence within a culture was one of the issues that most impacted Pastor Peter in our time together in Ethiopia. He saw discipleship modeled. He saw it lived out with all of the pastors we met with, as well as within our own team, and, as proved most impactful, when we began living it out with him. We wanted to know him, and we got to know him. And through those conversations, trust and friendship were born. The seeds of discipleship were planted, and it changed him eternally.

In Sodo, Ethiopia, when I talked to Peter that night, this was one of the most revelatory confessions he made to me: Within his church, even within his family, Peter didn't have anybody he could share with on a deep, meaningful level. But once he trusted us enough that the walls began to crumble and he could share and speak freely, seeing that we would do the same with him, his response was, "Oh, thank you, Lord, you have sent someone to share my burden."

This was the method of Jesus. This is what He commands us to do with each other as His disciples. This was what our staff and team modeled with Peter. And this is what he took to heart.

Carry each other's burdens, and in this way you will fulfill the law of Christ. —
Galatians 6:2, NIV

Hardly ever would you see a pastor in Africa stand before his congregation and admit that he was less than perfect. And yet, in Peter's church, and in the churches where he has influence, you are beginning to see just that.

That's one of the key markers we use: Is the pastor willing to "go there"? Is the pastor willing to risk that exposure and vulnerability by being open and transparent with his congregation, with his staff, and with his family?

I remember a conference down in Ecuador, modeling discipleship in a small group setting. Ten pastors from the local area were in my group and we had just hit this point of talking about being vulnerable—not just with each other, but with our congregations. Brows began to furrow despite their smiles. They began to talk with each other about how they loved being open and honest within this group, the burdens they now shared, and the safety and comfort they all felt. But then it hit them that they would have to recreate this same culture of transparency within their own churches; they would need to be real and authentic to their respective families, staffs, and congregations.

When this realization hit, they spent the next forty-five minutes, with little direction from me, on the question of, can we do this?

They knew that if they chose this path within their own communities, people could use such vulnerability, such admissions of weakness or fault, and likely hurt them, whether emotionally, physically, or monetarily. Something like what we were asking them to do, moreover what Jesus was asking of them, could very well cost them their jobs or their lives.

Eventually, by consensus, the group came to a decision. After weighing the risks and what God was asking, both the benefits and the danger, the group felt moved, overwhelmingly, to continue modeling what they had come to learn from our time together. They chose to pass on to their own families, and to their church families, the fruit of what they were seeing among themselves, in spite of any risk involved.

It was a beautiful moment to watch.

> *I have told you all this so that you may have peace in me. Here on earth you will have many trials and sorrows. But take heart,*

> *because I have overcome the world.* — John 16:33, NLT

To be sure, there are protective layers to this transparency. A pastor can be open to a certain extent to his congregation, to another level with his staff, to another level with his close advisors, and to an even deeper level with his most trusted friends and family.

It becomes the job of a coach, or the pastor himself, to see that he can create that kind of environment within his own team. This is the way God designed relationship, created within an environment of sharing and trust. Peter became convinced, through our own intentional modeling, that he could accomplish this same model with his own team, with his family, and, ultimately, with his congregation.

This was a big leap of faith. An indigenous pastor may feel safe sharing with a "visiting" team because they won't try to turn whatever is shared and use the information against him. But in his culture, as with the group from Ecuador and truly in every culture around the world, if he were to appear vulnerable to the wrong or untrusted people, he might be out of a job. He might even lose his life.

Trust Is Key

What makes all the difference is the open transparency our staff continues to show him whenever he visits here or we travel to Africa and when we communicate via social media, Skype, FaceTime, or by other means. Even then, what Peter and his staff continue to experience is that we are safe to share our "stuff" with—us with each other, and they with us—continually building a relationship based on a firm, safe foundation. We are living out, in real time, in real life, what it means to "go, and make disciples," and what it means to "love thy neighbor"—joining together the Great Commission and the Greatest Commandment. We are doing life together, just as Jesus did with His disciples.

> *"'Love the Lord your God with all your heart and with all your soul and with all your mind.' This is the first and greatest commandment. And the second is like it: 'Love your neighbor as yourself'...Therefore go and make disciples of all nations, baptizing them in the name of the Father and of the Son and of the Holy Spirit, and teaching them to obey everything I have commanded you. And surely I am with you always, to the very end of the age."*
> — Matthew 22:37–40; Matthew 28:19–20, NIV

Those of us who know him have begun to see a change in Peter, all traced back to the intentional friendship and the transparency and trust developed through our time of discipleship together. We have also seen a change in his family, in his congregation, and in many of the other pastors he has communicated with and trained.

Peter has taken Jesus's method of relational discipleship and began modeling it to everyone he meets, becoming the pastor Jesus was asking him to be, living as a true disciple and prayerfully selecting a few men in which to invest. He casts a vision for his church from the pulpit each Sunday, then lives it out himself during the week.

Through it all, Peter has been a great example of an intentional leader. He does not hurry the process but carries on, one step at a time, thoughtfully and prayerfully. His church has a steady pattern of growth, where small groups are continually forming and branching and people are being led to the Lord, and then being nurtured in a real relationship into mature disciples of Jesus.

> *A new commandment I give to you, that you love one another, even as I have loved you, that you also love one another. By this all men will know that you are My disciples, if you have love for one another.* — John 13:34–35, NASB

Over the last three years, Peter has not only impacted his own church, he has been given leadership over a ministry organization in Africa called Minevam. Through that opportunity, the Lord has used Peter to reach out to a great many of the pastors in his area, and even beyond. He now has a growing network of local ministers and churches. This network spreads across the entire country of Burundi and into six other countries of Africa, including the Congo, Rwanda, and Kenya. Throughout it all, we at RLM keep coming beside Pastor Peter, coaching and encouraging him, just as he does for his own staff as well as for those throughout the network of churches in Africa and beyond.

Peter has seen firsthand that relational discipleship is the direction of true growth, both within his church and within his own spiritual walk. Though it may have taken a pastoral team from halfway around the world to plant the seed, the idea has taken root and spread through the grace of God, and Peter's own personal commitment to follow and imitate the Master.

> *A pupil is not above his teacher; but everyone, after he has been fully trained, will be like his teacher.* — Luke 6:40, NASB

Peter would be the first to tell you that what he sees within those of us who continue to invest their time and friendship with him—as imperfect and a "work-in-progress" (Php 1:6) as we all are—is a living, convicting proof that this really is Jesus's model. There is so much that impacted him on a personal, intimate level that it could be no less than a supernatural, God-centered experience.

In other words, we were being what followers of Jesus were asked to be by the Messiah Himself, modeling what relational discipleship should look and sound and feel and act like.

Moreover, to be truly effective, and to make it relevant and impactful on a cultural and community level, someone like Peter has to be willing to not only teach the concepts but to be radically changed on a personal and intimate level, to transform his life and live it out with those he loves, and those in whom he has influence.

This is the difference between being a "trainee"—a mere seminar attender (or even a seminar presenter)—and being a contagious, radically changed disciple of Christ, one who can spread Jesus's message, His model, and live in relationship with others so that all can grow and flourish in the deep-seated love of Christ. What we showed Peter was something so radical and contagious, so counter-culture and so Jesus (making a disciple...), that he couldn't wait to pass it on to his church, his coworkers, and his family (...who makes disciples).

In Peter's case, it became his goal to build a strong leadership team and a close inner circle, all of them willing to risk crossing this cultural hurdle—what, in actuality, is a human nature hurdle—so they could live out this radical concept, growing in intentional relationship with each other, and with Jesus.

And so he has, proving that God has certainly watered Peter's initial seed of desire for making disciples who make disciples.

Two years after attending his first DiscipleShift training in Ethiopia, we received a note from Pastor Peter to our staff at RLM. Here's what Peter had to say about a recent discipleship training he facilitated within his own country, and of the explosive growth possible through relational discipleship. The English may be a little rough, but his heart is crystal clear and his excitement is palpable:

> *Dear beloved in Christ,*
> *We are ready started the training, almost 50 pastors and 30 youth leaders are attended the seminar. I thank God because the teachings given them before have found the fruits. Today, in our country, we have almost 200 small groups, praise be to the Lord.*
> *I continue to encourage them and I believe the small groups will grow and extending in many places.*

> *The pastors from Tanzania joined us in training, 7 small groups are started.*
> *Thank you for your prayer and support.*
>
> *Greet all of you for us,*
> *Pastor Peter*

God Himself sees the true growth possible under relational discipleship. Not only that, you can take heart that, within His Word, He has promised to water this method, Jesus's method, and to make it blossom and flourish:

> *And I saw between the throne (with the four living creatures) and the elders a Lamb standing, as if slain, having seven horns and seven eyes, which are the seven Spirits of God, sent out into all the earth. And He came and took the book out of the right hand of Him who sat on the throne. When He had taken the book, the four living creatures and the twenty-four elders fell down before the Lamb, each one holding a harp and golden bowls full of incense, which are the prayers of the saints. And they sang a new song, saying, "Worthy are You to take the book and to break its seals;* **for You were slain, and purchased for God with Your blood men from every tribe and tongue and people and nation. You have made them to be a kingdom and priests to our God; and they will reign upon the earth.**" — Revelation 5:6–10, NASB (emphasis mine)

> **This gospel of the kingdom shall be preached in the whole world as a testimony to all the nations,** *and then the end will come.* — Matthew 24:14, NASB (emphasis mine)

Bible verses to consider

Matthew 28:16-20

John 15:15-16

2 Corinthians 5:17

John 14:12

John 16:33

John 13:34-35

Luke 6:40

Philippians 2:6

Revelation 5:6-10

Matthew 24:14

Study questions for further discussion

*How does relationship (using the Biblical definition) tie into Biblical discipleship?

*What did you learn from this chapter about your relationship with God? With others?

*What impacted you the most about Pastor Peter's story?

Disciples Unleashed

Chapter 4
Key Pastors Are Contagious:
Reproducing Jesus's Model Church by Church

The next ring in the target is all about Jesus's multiplication principle: that His followers (as His disciples) who are making more disciples will multiply and bear much fruit.

> *And the things you have heard me say in the presence of many witnesses entrust to reliable people who will also be qualified to teach others.* — 2 Timothy 2:2, NIV

> *"I am the vine; you are the branches. If you remain in me and I in you, you will bear much fruit; apart from me you can do nothing. 6 If you do not remain in me, you are like a branch that is thrown away and withers; such branches are picked up, thrown into the fire and burned. 7 If you remain in me and my words remain in you, ask whatever you wish, and it will be done for you. 8 This is to my Father's glory, that you bear much fruit, showing yourselves to be my disciples."* — John 15:5–8, NIV

> *"...you will receive power when the Holy Spirit comes on you; and you will be my witnesses in Jerusalem, and in all Judea and Samaria, and to the ends of the earth."* — Acts 1:8, NIV

These verses paint a picture of Jesus's plan to reach the whole world for Himself by making disciples who make disciples. Jesus knew something very important: True discipleship is intentional, reproducible, and contagious.

All around the world we see cultural walls crumbling and denominational barriers dissolving, where pastors, staff, families, and congregants have joined together to focus on following Jesus into a disciple-making relationship, making disciples who in turn are following Jesus and making disciples.

Pastors from around the globe and from a wide range of differing denominations are seeing the success in returning to Jesus's method of relational discipleship. Through firsthand experience, or by seeing the success of their neighboring churches, many of these pastors are coming to their own aha moments. And rightly so. There is a fundamental cultural shift taking place within the church, and God is the one bringing this to pass using pastors and congregants of disciple-making churches to spread it to other pastors and to other churches.

I believe it's high time we sit up and take notice!

The Tension between Head and Heart

When the staff of Real Life Ministries first set out in creating our DiscipleShift weekends, one of the most difficult aspects we encountered was in trying to put into words this thing we've been describing, this method of relational discipleship. What Jesus is asking of us and what we're trying to bring the church back in line with is not a "program" and it's not a set "doctrine"; it truly is a way of living. It means an intentional shift in the way we live our lives and live out our faith, and in the way we interact with others, whether they are newly exploring the claims of Christ or more mature followers of the living God.

As I mentioned in the Introduction, many people have come to DiscipleShift expecting nothing more than the latest, greatest plan for guaranteed church growth—a bullet-point list or diagramed chart that, when followed, magically begins to put warm bodies in seats and tithes in coffers. I hope you are beginning to see that truly living out relational discipleship is not about church growth, because Jesus wasn't interested in church growth as we commonly define it these days (i.e., church attendance and growth, dynamic programs and worship, and so on—if you don't believe me, read John chapter 6 again sometime.)

This is about bringing people to a renewed understanding of the method and message of Jesus Christ—not only what He said, but how He chose to live it out. Jesus was not interested in simply amassing a group of followers. He was interested in redemption, of making old things new again, and in bringing dead faith back to life. Jesus was interested in bringing light into a darkened world. His method of living out His message is about being a light so attractive that people can't help but ask what it is that you've got, and how they can get it. This isn't something you can list, nor is it something you can merely read or check off as you complete the "steps."

The Pharisees in first-century Jerusalem made the same misguided assumption. No one would deny that these guys had a thorough knowledge of the law, of the do's and don'ts, and of the checklists. Of anyone, the Pharisees had the "law" down, all 600-plus rules. Then this radical rabbi, this carpenter's son, this Jesus fellow, shows up and says, you're missing the point! (Actually, I think He called them "hypocrites" and "you brood of vipers," but I digress.)

I feel a great many pastors understand the message of Scripture. We all know the Scriptures say love your neighbor. We all know the Scriptures say to assemble together, and to be united as one. This is knowledge at the head level and is quite honestly a vital, necessary tool in both absorbing and furthering God's Word and His kingdom.

But...

What's missing is not so much an understanding of the message; what's missing is an understanding of the method. What does loving your neighbor, assembling together, and being united as one actually look like?

"You have heard it said..., but I say..."

Jesus was completely aware that the Jewish elect had Scriptural teachings fully in hand on a knowledge basis—at a head level. But what He cared about, what He calls the Pharisees on, what He preached on the mountainside, on the streets, in the synagogues, and how He lived among His disciples, is how He took that knowledge, and how we take this knowledge today, into a heart-level understanding: knowing it, yes, but living it as well. This is truly what Jesus cares about for His church and His disciples (in other words, us). This is spiritual maturity: to love

God well and to love others well; to actually live out, through the transforming power of God's Spirit, the Greatest Commandment as written in Matthew 22.

When we, whether as individuals or as a collective church body, choose to reflect Jesus to the world—to live with one another in relational discipleship—it is inevitable that we will become attractive to that same world. People will notice. Whether they choose to accept or partake of our offer of relationship is up to them, but they will notice.

> *"A new command I give you: Love one another. As I have loved you, so you must love one another. By this everyone will know that you are my disciples, if you love one another."*
> — John 13:34–35, NIV

On the flip side, when we try to out-argue the world, or convince the world of the reality of our doctrine, it is not received nearly as well (if at all). Oh sure, our behavior is noticed, but not in any kind of attractive or enticing fashion. When we do this, we are not so much a shining light as we are, as the Apostle Paul puts it, a "resounding gong" or a "clanging cymbal." Paul also puts it this way, in his first letter to the Corinthians:

> *So whether you eat or drink, or whatever you do, do it all for the glory of God. Don't give offense to Jews or Gentiles or the church of God. I, too, try to please everyone in everything I do. I don't just do what is best for me; I do what is best for others so that many may be saved.* ***And you should imitate me, just as I imitate Christ.*** — 1 Corinthians 10:31–11:1, NLT (emphasis mine)

Even one person can make a difference. One person can put that first chink into cultural walls. One person can begin laying the bridge that crosses denominational barriers. One person can begin living their life in such a way that they draw people in, making a difference in their family, in their neighborhood, in their church—a difference so attractive that people can't help but ask what it is that they've got, and how they can get it as well.

Let me tell you two stories, one Biblical and one from a friend of mine, illustrating just what I mean.

The Woman at the Well

Most of us are familiar with the encounter between Jesus and the Samaritan woman at Jacob's well outside of Sychar.

> *So [Jesus] came to a town in Samaria called Sychar, near the plot of ground Jacob had given to his son Joseph. Jacob's well was there, and Jesus, tired as he was from the journey, sat down by the well. It was about noon. When a Samaritan woman came to draw water, Jesus said to her, "Will you give me a drink?" (His disciples had gone into the town to buy food.) The Samaritan woman said to him, "You are a Jew and I am a Samaritan woman. How can you ask me for a drink?" (For Jews do not associate with Samaritans.)* — John 4:5–9, NIV

She comes to the well and questions His intentions because of a centuries-old clash of cultures.

Hundreds of years prior, after the death of King Solomon, the people of Israel split into two distinct regions. The ten tribes to the north lived in the area known as Israel, and their capital was Samaria. The two tribes to the south, Judah and Benjamin, lived in the area called Judah, and their capital was Jerusalem.

Around 724 B.C., Assyria overpowered the northern kingdom, and most of the people of Israel who survived were taken captive and assimilated into the Assyrian population, scattered throughout various Assyrian cities around the known world, or non-Jewish populations were brought in and intermixed with the people of Israel. It was a strategic move on the part of Assyria because over time, the very identity and culture of the Jewish populace began to crumble as they absorbed more and more of the cultural rites and rituals of the Assyrians surrounding them.

This was the foundation and cause of the bitter hatred between Jews, who remained "pure" in culture and belief, and the Samaritans, those of "mixed" blood—the Jews who had been assimilated by the Assyrians—who, over time, adopted a pastiche of religious and cultural practices, including the construction of a temple of worship on Mount Gerizim outside of Sychar, the "mountain" the woman at the well speaks of during her conversation with Jesus.

After all this history, it is no wonder the woman was surprised that Jesus would stoop to talk with her. And yet, He goes further. He begins to tell her about her sordid past (of five ex-husbands, and currently living with a man out of wedlock), knowledge that she admits He should not have known unless He were a prophet. Jesus goes on to tell her He is that and so much more.

> *The woman said, "I know that Messiah" (called Christ) "is coming. When he comes, he will explain everything to us."*
> *Then Jesus declared, "I, the one speaking to you—I am he."* — John 4:25–26, NIV

At this, the woman leaves her watering jar and runs back to the village to tell everyone who it is that she has met.

> *So when the Samaritans came to him, they urged him to stay with them, and he stayed two days. And because of his words many more became believers. They said to the woman, "We no longer believe just because of what you said; now we have heard for ourselves, and we know that this man really is the Savior of the world."*
> — John 4:40–42, NIV

I struggled with this section of the passage for quite some time when I was first studying the Bible. It seemed like almost a slight against the woman when the villagers said, "We no longer believe just because of what you said." But as I began to consider this statement, I thought about my own children and how I would love nothing more than to hear, "Now we believe for ourselves, and not just because you've been making us go to church." In other words, the villagers heard at the head level from the woman, but Jesus affected them at the heart level.

One woman made a difference to an entire village. Her testimony brought people to Jesus, and "many...from that town believed in him because of the woman's testimony...and because of his words many more became believers" (John 4:39, 41).

The Schoolteacher of St. John's

As you can see from stories in the previous chapters and from this story of the woman at the well, God's Word, and the words and life of Jesus, tend to have a ripple effect upon those who hear them, taking them not only at the head level but into the hearts and into their lives.

The story of Richard Aitken, vicar of St. John's Anglican parish, in Invercargill, New Zealand, is another example of just such a ripple effect.

Richard was a school teacher and then headmaster of schools in Auckland and Dunedin, New Zealand. Growing up in the Anglican Church, he was a very serious young man who, in his late teens, came to a strong faith of his own. Throughout his school career, Richard always felt the calling in some aspect toward a return to the Anglican Church. Fortunately, at the time, the church was looking for pastors, especially bi-vocational pastors (those who held another position as well as the clergy). Unfortunately, many of the churches throughout New Zealand at that time were in decline, losing congregants through a growing cultural indifference or to the aging of the attending populace.

Still, for Richard the calling remained and, despite the hardship to his family of giving up a full-time career in the schools, he began his studies in seminary. Through contacts within the Anglican Church, he came to an agreement with the local diocese that he could do online courses for the majority of his studies and they would give him a small parish, where he would come to be the vicar.

This church, the Anglican Parish of St. John, had a congregation of about thirty people. His instructions were, in essence, to take these worshipers and this beautiful, several-hundred-years-old church which seated over 500 people and "love the people, but put the congregation to sleep, peacefully." In other words, we know this is a dying church. Let's let it rest in peace.

Most of the congregants were in their late sixties or older. The sermons up to that time were very liturgical—long, flowing robes and solemn words from an elevated platform.

One day Richard was browsing through a church bookstore in Invercargill and, rounding a corner, he bumped a certain book off of a merchandise table. The book happened to be Real Life Ministries' pastor Jim Putman's book, *Church is a Team Sport*. With his interest piqued— a voracious reader, Richard happens to like both religion and sports—he purchased the book.

Jim's writing planted the first seeds of what a church could, and should, be and how Jesus designed and modeled what church should look like. Through research, Richard began to communicate with Real Life and, eventually, attended one of our DiscipleShift experiences.

He saw modeled here Jesus's method of relational discipleship. He attended small groups where people opened up, were vulnerable, and were safe. He saw genuine sharing and caring. And, even in his brief stay, he saw the transforming power of discipleship and the maturity that was possible, both for the church and the individual, through authentic relationship.

Richard returned to New Zealand, in awe and in wonder of how he could take the model shown to him and apply it to a congregation of sixty- and seventy-year-olds, a congregation used to a lifetime of liturgy, solemnity, and status quo.

He started at the beginning, with his own family, living out discipleship with his wife and children. Their relationship prospered, serving each other and serving the church. The kids had a growing interest and knowledge of the Gospel. Before long, a few parishioners began to notice and, through that piqued curiosity, Richard planted a few seeds of relational discipleship. Soon, he began his first small group. One led to two, and then three.

But not all the seeds landed on fertile ground, at least not at first. One group of ladies that Richard thought might be interested in forming a small group outright refused, saying they would never be a part of a small group. This was a concept of relationship that fell nowhere near their level of comfort and familiarity.

However, Richard's custodian had recently quit without much notice, and he found himself needing help in keeping up with their beautiful (and large) church building. This same group of ladies decided to volunteer their time to clean the church building. They were not interested in wasting time in a small group, but they were happy to spend it tidying up around the parish. Richard was beyond grateful.

Over time, he began serving them coffee, offering "a brief break" in their cleaning duties. The ladies thought this was lovely.

Then, a few weeks later, Richard asked if he might bring out something from God's Word that they could discuss while they sipped their drinks and as they went about their duties afterward around the church. The ladies thought this was very considerate of Richard, and readily agreed.

Gradually, over the following months, Richard let them in on a little secret...

They had become a "small group"! (Though, to this day, they prefer to call it a bible-reading and church-cleaning reflection-and-discussion group).

Now, years on, these ladies still meet, and Richard still joins them on occasion, and a few ladies have invited a few more—still under the guise of cleaning the church, of course.

Also in that time, more small groups have begun to form and a few have branched, forming more. Richard's congregation has since grown from thirty to over eighty now, complete with a children's ministry and youth and young adult programs.

It hasn't all been smooth sailing. There are still a few of the older congregants, still attending St. John's, who have not conceded to joining a small group. And that's been okay with Richard; he hasn't pushed. He has seen, and is living proof, of the benefit of living in relationship as designed by Jesus for His church. But Richard also concedes that only the Holy Spirit can truly change the hearts and minds of His followers. And change He has; the majority of St. John's congregation have revived the parish, reenergizing their passion for God's Word and for Jesus's method and message. They have invested their time and lives for each other, and begun experiencing the fruit of relational discipleship, even in the twilight of life.

Now they believe for themselves, not just because Richard told them what relational discipleship could do for them. Even an inexperienced, untrained vicar can come in to a dying parish, modeling Jesus's method of relationship, first with his family, then with an interested few, even with some ladies interested in nothing more than a clean church, and draw the attention of the surrounding community.

The interest that Richard sparked continues to spread as pastors from surrounding communities are beginning to take notice and ask questions. Richard and our staff have begun meeting with other pastors from Invercargill, coaching and encouraging them in Jesus's relational model. Richard has also taken us to another town, Dunedin, a few hours away, where we have had the opportunity to meet with a group of over twenty church leaders from that area, mostly but not all Anglican. In fact, Richard continues to meet with these pastors, encouraging and coaching them, answering questions and engaging in relational discipleship even within this group of seasoned vicars, as interest continues to surge outward.

One such pastor is Dr. Adam Dodds from the Elim church in Dunedin. Adam and his team had been searching for that elusive "next step" for their congregation. The Elim church network is one of the fastest growing Christian organizations in New Zealand, with a congregation of over a thousand members, and is part of a network of churches throughout both New Zealand and Australia. Through Richard's model and work, we were able to go back and do a full DiscipleShift[6] which included the entire staff of the Elim church as well as other leadership training which included over forty of their small group leaders. These people were already fulfilling the call to reach the lost, including a huge outreach to the local college campus, and it became our job, and Richard's, to show them how to create and maintain relational discipleship as the logical next step in bringing up disciples who can then create more disciples.

Adam Dodds has really taken to heart Jesus's method of disciple making, continuing to work with Richard and coaching his own staff. Adam has also been in contact with several other Elim denominational churches, and is laying the groundwork to take relational discipleship throughout New Zealand.

Richard's contacts within the Anglican churches are also showing a growing interest in what they are seeing within Richard's parish and the fire that has caught on in the surrounding communities, all springing forth from one Anglican vicar who was asked to quietly "put to sleep" his local parish.

The size of the church doesn't matter in relational discipleship; it depends much more on the faithfulness of the congregation and staff, and the willingness to embrace Jesus's method as well as His message, living out the true model of relationship that God desires for His followers.

The key thing about Richard is not his natural position of influence, but that God has given Richard favor as he has continues to walk out relational discipleship personally. His

---

[6] DiscipleShift (technically DiscipleShift 1) is a two-day relational experience designed to challenge all who attend on a personal level in three different areas: Head, Heart & Hands. DiscipleShift's interactive, relational environment gives teams an opportunity to rediscover Jesus's message of discipleship; to be involved in (and experience) His method of disciple making through modeling intentional leadership; to build and lead effective teams (whether staff or home groups) in relational environments through understanding the value of Biblical storytelling and effective small group facilitation; and to promote alignment in our core beliefs, moving the entire church toward a common, reproducible purpose—to make disciples who can then make disciples. For more information: http://www.reallifeministries.com/discipleshift1/

marriage has been renewed and revitalized. His children are being intentionally discipled. And his church has been forever changed.

The Anglican diocese in southern New Zealand has around 70 churches, and yet only two of these churches are growing in any manner. Richard's is one of them. Now, the diocese Anglican board has asked for Richard's input into how he is seeing such against-the-grain growth of his church.

No, it may not be about church growth, certainly not as it is commonly viewed in the Christian world today. But living out Jesus's model of relationship is contagious. One person can make a difference. One person can influence change in his or her church, family, and community. One person can put that first chink into cultural walls and begin laying a bridge that crosses denominational barriers. Richard Aitken began living his life in such a way that drew the attention of the Invercargill community, the Anglican Church, and beyond. Living out Jesus's model of relationship made an infectious difference in his own family, in his growing congregation, and soon, in all of New Zealand.

Bible verses to consider

2 Timothy 2:2

John 15:1-8

Acts 1:8

Matthew 16:15-18

1 Cor. 10:31-11:1

John 4:5-9

John 4:25-26

John 4:39-41

Study questions for further discussion

*How, Biblically speaking, do "head knowledge" and "heart change" interact?

*What do you learn from Pastor Richard's story that you can personally apply in your own life?

Disciples Unleashed

Chapter 5
Creating the Biblical Model in "Your" Church

> *They devoted themselves to the apostles' teaching and to fellowship, to the breaking of bread and to prayer. Everyone was filled with awe at the many wonders and signs performed by the apostles. All the believers were together and had everything in common. They sold property and possessions to give to anyone who had need. Every day they continued to meet together in the temple courts. They broke bread in their homes and ate together with glad and sincere hearts, praising God and enjoying the favor of all the people. And the Lord added to their number daily those who were being saved.*
> — Acts 2:42–47, NIV

The Early Church

Now we come to the fifth ring of our ever-narrowing target: the creation of a Biblical church culture.

There are certain characteristics of action and attitude, ones that manifest themselves both inwardly in the believer and outwardly to the community, that can define and set apart a certain kind of church body. These characteristics lead out with an assured selflessness, with empathy and compassion, and through a widespread attitude of love and grace displayed through intentional actions of service and outreach.

It's not evangelizing. It's not proselytizing.

It's called being the church or, more precisely, being *Jesus's* church. This is what it looks like as we enter the next ring of our target, built on the stand of Jesus's model of relationship with His disciples and with us:

> *Consequently, you are no longer foreigners and strangers, but fellow citizens with God's people and also members of his household, built on the foundation of the*

> *apostles and prophets, with Christ Jesus himself as the chief cornerstone.* **In him the whole building is joined together and rises to become a holy temple in the Lord. And in him you too are being built together to become a dwelling in which God lives by his Spirit**. — Ephesians 2:19–22, NIV (emphasis mine)

> *All the believers were one in heart and mind. No one claimed that any of their possessions was their own, but they shared everything they had. With great power the apostles continued to testify to the resurrection of the Lord Jesus. And God's grace was so powerfully at work in them all that there were no needy persons among them.* — Acts 4:32–34a, NIV

The moment you walk through the front doors, many of the characteristics of intentional, relational discipleship are easy to spot within a congregation. What you will often find is that everyone you meet seems to be of one mind and purpose, enjoying themselves and the friends and family surrounding them. They have "everything in common" and everyone seems to unite behind each other—providing for needs, sharing and expounding on the Word, and meeting together outside the walls of the church—and the overall atmosphere is dynamic and growing. These "bodies of Christ" seem to "enjoy the favor of all the people," and through this fellowship "the Lord adds to their number."

This is what we are beginning to see more and more in churches throughout the United States and around the world, because these churches are beginning to live out Jesus and the apostles' model of relational discipleship, the model carried out and nurtured throughout the first chapters of Acts.

Each time I am introduced to a new church community—wherever it is, in any part of the world—I always pray to find the seeds of interest in becoming more aligned with this early church culture; a culture devoted to prayer, one that meets together in both the local building and the homes of its members, and of their friends and neighbors; and a culture in which all people care for each other, for the spiritual growth of their families, and the spiritual awakening of their community.

So the question becomes this: How does the church pastor and leadership create this type of culture within their respective churches?

The reality faced daily by these key leaders is that, just like a sports team that wins a championship, a church doesn't automatically open its doors at that level of performance, nor does the teamwork and determination necessary to achieve that status continue on, automatically or effortlessly, once that level is achieved.

The stark contrast between the culture of so many churches worldwide and that of the church culture seen in Acts is so important to distinguish because when someone new to the church, or new to Christianity for that matter, shows up at the doorway, they are going to feel a culture within the foyer or sanctuary, among the people who call this place their church home, that speaks to these newcomers at a heart level. They are going to feel a culture that says either, "Hey, I'm glad I'm here. The worship is good. The message is solid and Biblical. I think this is a church we could attend. We'll come back next Sunday," or they will feel one that says, "Okay, there is an expectation here. There is an excitement here. There is an atmosphere here. I'm not just attending this church; they want me to be a part of their team. Yes, there is good worship and a good message, but each member is also being equipped and expected to become a disciple who makes disciples."

Within the second example, no one is leaving their spiritual growth solely to the pastor. No one came through the doors in order to hide or to blend in, or just to check a box that they came to church on Sunday. Inevitably the result of this second type of culture is a believer who says, "I want to play a part of this church, because the church wants me to play a part."

Don't misunderstand me here. Both cultures offer solid platforms for making churchgoers hungry for the Word of God. Yet the difference—and this is the key foundation that we emphasize here at Real Life Ministries and through our DiscipleShift process—is a difference of building up a congregation that either attends church ("We'll come back next Sunday") or one that is committed to becoming the church ("I want to play a part...because the church wants me to play a part, and Jesus's plan is that I play a part"). I think God makes it quite clear through the Apostle Paul which culture He would see His church gravitate toward.

> *For we are God's handiwork, created in Christ Jesus to do good works, which God prepared in advance for us to do.* — Ephesians 2:10, NIV

As I said, this second culture is the culture we strive for at Real Life Ministries, and one that we see as the Biblical model that Jesus and His apostles lived and taught.

This is a culture of participation, not merely attendance.

Jesus modeled this culture to His disciples throughout His teaching ministry (for example, Matthew 28:18–20; Luke 10:1; and John 13:3–17). This culture is one boldly proclaimed by the apostles and lived out in the first several chapters of Acts. This culture is also well described by Paul a little later on in his letter to the Ephesians:

> *So Christ himself gave the apostles, the prophets, the evangelists, the pastors and teachers, to equip his people for works of service, so that the body of Christ may be built up until we all reach unity in the faith and in the knowledge of the Son of God and become mature, attaining to the whole measure of the fullness of Christ.*
>
> *Then we will no longer be infants, tossed back and forth by the waves, and blown here and there by every wind of teaching and by the cunning and craftiness of people in their deceitful scheming. Instead, speaking the truth in love, we will grow to become in every respect*

the mature body of him who is the head, that is, Christ. From him the whole body, joined and held together by every supporting ligament, grows and builds itself up in love, as each part does its work. — Ephesians 4:11–16, NIV

Paul tells us that we are to live out this culture of relational discipleship so that "the body of Christ may be built up reaching unity in the faith." Why? Because when we do, we become mature believers, steadfast in our faith, in our love, and in our acts of reaching out to one another in service, so that we can attain "to the whole measure of the fullness of Christ." What that means is that we become total and complete examples of the light and life of Christ to a world that so desperately needs to be shown, with hands and heart, the "good news" of Jesus's saving grace. This is what we long to see when we talk with church leaders about the discipleship process, and this is what each church should want people to feel as they walk through the doors—that feeling of connection and that they are wanted, not merely for their attendance but because, to the church, each member is a vital part of ministry, outreach, relationship, and discipling.

Real Life Ministries did not invent this culture. We did not discover anything new. Our senior pastor, Jim Putman, has said, "God is doing what He is doing through RLM in North Idaho to show that any rock head can be a disciple who makes disciples; we just have to follow His model."

At RLM, we don't do this perfectly, and sometimes we still don't even do it well. We mess up just like Jesus's original disciples did. But we don't give up when we blow it. We go back to the model and back to the One who created the model, and we keep following Him, being transformed and walking in His mission. That is what intentionality looks like in the discipleship process, because this is what Jesus's disciples do!

Pastor Christian

One such church where this type of culture is lived out on a daily basis is in the small tourist community of Playa del

Carmen, an hour's drive south of Cancun, Mexico, on the Riviera Maya.

The church is called Compañerismo de la Riviera Maya, located five kilometers from the heart of Playa del Carmen, and the senior pastor is a man named Christian Carballo.

Born in Chetumal and raised in Cancun, Christian is a native of the Mexican Caribbean and the second of three children. He began what he thought would be a lifetime career in the tourism industry at the age of seventeen, working his way through several positions in the operation of hotels, though his passion lay mainly in the area of sales and marketing.

During this time he also began attending a church in Playa del Carmen pastored by American missionary Doug Millar along with his wife and missions partner, Darla. Doug recognized the enthusiasm and drive of the young man from Cancun and began investing more and more of his time with Christian, mentoring him and soon bringing him on staff as associate pastor.

At the time, Christian was still working in the hotel and tourism industry, and about the time he was named associate pastor, he also attained the position of vice president of groups and incentive sales for a well-known hotel chain. This promotion seemed to be the culmination of his hard work and success within the tourist industry, and by the world's standards, he appeared to have it all. But the job required him to move to Miami, Florida, a move that took him away from his family and his church. This was not to last for long.

After a year of going back and forth from Miami to Playa del Carmen, God made obvious the calling He had given Christian since an early age. Christian recognized that the most important thing in his life was his relationship with God, with his wife Abimelec (Aby), and with his family. It was an epiphany that would change his life. Soon after, he quit his job in Miami and returned to Playa del Carmen, where he became associate pastor for the church on a full-time basis.

Once there, the church model that Christian abided by was one familiar to many of us: there was expository preaching, where the pastor spoke the Word of God and the congregation listened; there was enthusiastic worship; and there was an enjoyable Sunday school. But there was no real fruit of intentional, relational discipleship. Members faithfully came to church, but there was no feeling of "being a part." There was also no urgency in "being the church" within the community, and there was no feeling of need to gather together outside the walls of the building once the service was finished.

Pastor Doug expressed his frustrations to Christian, his apprentice and associate, about the lack of growth within the church—both in the numbers and in spiritual maturity. Attendance would grow and shrink with the passing seasons, and divisions and splits would occur, but there was never any sustained growth; many of those who attended felt their commitment to God was met at the conclusion of services on Sunday.

Through friends in the States, Doug heard about what was happening with Real Life Ministries in the small town of Post Falls, Idaho—how the church there had grown from a small handful of families to thousands of members in less than ten years' time—and eventually he came to a DiscipleShift, bringing along his wife Darla along with him, as well as inviting Christian and Aby.

The weekend they spent with our team, and several other church leaders from around the country, impacted Christian and his wife immensely, but Doug, though impacted, did not see the relational model we were talking about as something that would work. He could see the Biblical basis of Jesus's design, but this discipleship culture was not something he felt was "doable" within his church. What we were proposing was a long step from what he felt his congregation was ready for or comfortable with; it meant a radical shift in the mindset of his churchgoers, one he was unsure they would be willing to embrace eagerly.

But to his credit, and even though he was reluctant, upon their return Doug gave Christian his blessing and permission to undertake the discipleship model with a few of the young man's staff and close friends. Over the next few years, Christian began to personally live out Jesus's model of relational discipleship, first with his family and then with his closest associates.

In 2014, Doug and Darla Millar stepped back from Compañerismo de la Riviera Maya, continuing their vision of outreach and missionary work to the impoverished communities along the Mayan peninsula. At his leaving, Doug appointed Christian as his successor as senior pastor.

By this time, Christian was well into the discipleship process with some of his closest associates. They became interested in pursuing the Biblical discipleship model within their own families after seeing how Christian had been living out Jesus's model within his own life, how his family had grown closer to each other, and deeper into their relationship with Christ.

Christian began in earnest to train up these young men within his church, becoming more intentionally involved in their lives and careers and discipling them as he had seen Jesus live it out with His own disciples and as the Apostle Paul had lived it out with Timothy:

> *Timothy, my dear son, be strong through the grace that God gives you in Christ Jesus. You have heard me teach things that have been confirmed by many reliable witnesses. Now teach these truths to other trustworthy people who will be able to pass them on to others.* — 2 Timothy 2:1–2, NLT

These men soon became some of the key leaders in Christian's church—small group leaders and staff—initiating a total shift in the culture and attitude of the church. Initial fears that the congregation would be reluctant to such change proved unfounded. Through Christian's leadership and guidance, Compañerismo de la Riviera Maya evolved into a place to become connected and involved in the lives of friends and neighbors, and in the community as a whole, doing life together, seeing each other through births and deaths, financial crises, and so on, wherever there was need. In essence, what Christian and his staff were able to do was shift the church body's focus from a "go to church" culture to a "be the church" culture.

> *All the believers were one in heart and mind. No one claimed that any of their*

possessions was their own, but they shared everything they had. With great power the apostles continued to testify to the resurrection of the Lord Jesus. And God's grace was so powerfully at work in them all that there were no needy persons among them. For from time to time those who owned land or houses sold them, brought the money from the sales and put it at the apostles' feet, and it was distributed to anyone who had need. — Acts 4:32–35, NIV

Through the intentional vision casting of Christian, and living out what it means to be a disciple-making church as seen throughout the beginning of Acts, there has been a growing and dynamic outreach in individual lives. Families have been changed, people are coming to know the Lord, friends are being invited, and there is spiritual growth going on as never seen before. To arrive at the church now, you can just feel the change in attitude and atmosphere, one that is now full of life and vitality.

Recently, Christian confided in me that one of the church's biggest challenges today is in raising up leaders within the small group networks in order to keep up with the demand of growth so the groups they now have can branch and continue in the process of raising disciples who make disciples.

I have to chuckle whenever he says this, and he always smiles as well. Honestly, of the many issues a church could have, this is a wonderful "challenge" to have to face.

Bible verses to consider

Acts 2:42-47

Ephesians 2:19-22

Acts 4:32-37

Ephesians 2:10

John 13:34-35

Ephesians 4:11-16

2 Timothy 2:1-2

Study questions for further discussion

*How does the Biblical model of church, as laid out in the first chapters of Acts and others, differ from what you observe in your own church?

*What can you do, personally, in your life to help create a true Biblical culture in your church?

*What do you learn from Christian's story?

Chapter 6
Impacting Your Family, Your Friends, and Your Leadership Team

As we focus more on what it means to live out Jesus's model of relational discipleship, first from the worldwide impact to countries being impacted, to this Biblical discipleship model being sustainable and reproducible, I want to talk about another pastor doing some amazing work within his leadership and family. His name is Praveen Chand, and his story involves the next ring of our target—seeking out ways to invite in and impact church leadership and family.

Indo-Fijians and Native Fijians
What's in a Name?

As we key in on Praveen's story, let's return for a moment to the island nation of Fiji and dive a little further into its culture and history. Praveen is an Indo-Fijian, born and raised in a Hindu family who can trace their ancestry back to the era of indentured servitude among the sugar cane plantations of the late nineteenth century.

As I wrote in previous chapters, like most societies around the world, there are many distinct cultural layers within the Fijian community, but the two primary ethnicities are the native Fijians (those of Melanesian or Polynesian ancestry and indigenous to the islands) and the Indo-Fijians.

Indo-Fijians are Fijian citizens, numbering almost 38 percent of the island's population according to a 2007 census, who are either fully or partially of North Indian ancestry. Indo-Fijians are mostly descended from indentured laborers, called *girmitiyas* or *girmit*, brought to the islands by Fiji's British colonial rulers between 1879 and 1916 to work on Fiji's sugar cane plantations, selling themselves to plantation owners or sea captains for a period of time in order to escape the abject poverty of their own country.

Indo-Fijians are as proud of their dual heritage and of their descendants' desire to rise above the circumstances of their homeland, as they are proud to call themselves Fijian. Some native Fijians though take issue with the fact that these people, though valued and contributing members of their communities are not true "natives." Even the name "Indo-Fijian" is ripe with controversy.

According to an article in the *Hindustan Times* written in August of 2006, Joné Navakamocea, Minister of State for National Planning in the Qarase government at the time, called for the use of the term "Indo-Fijian" to be officially banned, saying the term was "unacceptable" and that Indo-Fijians should be referred to only as "Indians." He alleged that the Indo-Fijian term was coined by Indian academics in Fiji to "Fijianise" their Indian ethnicity, undermining their indigenous rights. Navakamocea lost office in the 2006 military coup when the army accused the Qarase government of anti-Fijian Indian racism.[7]

Pastor Praveen

These are just a few of the hurdles that Praveen faces in trying to build and nourish intentional relationships among his leaders, among his congregation, and within his community, simply because of who he is and the family he happened to be born into.

Praveen is counted among those proud of their Indian ancestry. In fact, at a young age he started out his religious life as a Hindu priest, practicing Hinduism at a deep and personal level, including sacrificial offerings and what we Westerners might consider "witch doctor" type practices.

In his late teens, Praveen met a Christian pastor from a church in Sigatoka, Fiji, named Simon Gounder. Simon saw an interest and sincerity in the young man and began teaching and mentoring Praveen, instructing him Scriptural truth and introducing him to the grace and sacrifice of Jesus Christ. Soon after, Praveen gave his life to the Lord, but was the only one in his family to do so. For years the rest of his relatives shunned

---

[7] "Ban the term Indo-Fijian: Minister," *Hindustan Times*, 5 August 2006.

and rejected him, but Praveen pressed on in his decision to become a Christian pastor, further straining the tensions rumbling within his family.

Faithfully, as the years passed, Praveen continued pursuing his family through patience and kindness, talking with relatives when he could, reasoning out his beliefs in contrast to his Hindu upbringing, and pointing out the way of Biblical truths. Now, thanks in no small part to his patient persistence, many of Praveen's family are also believers.

Around 2010, Praveen moved to New Zealand to delve deeper into his pastoral career. A few years later, Simon was invited by his church administration to move to the United States, and the two men's careers seemed to follow their own paths.

Then, within a year or two into Simon's career in the States, Praveen was asked by Simon to assume leadership of his former church in Sigatoka. It seemed, in Simon's absence, that issues had arisen within the church, driving fissures into the relationships of staff and families. There were accusations of embezzlement by some of the leadership and attitudes had become passive and apathetic amidst a dwindling congregation, and above it all lay an inherent tension of mistrust between those who chose to remain.

Nonetheless, Praveen agreed to assume the position of senior pastor, but tension and disillusionment hung on. After all, it was a previous appointee of Simon who had been responsible for much of the mismanagement accusations feeding into the church's frustration. A lot of key families did not want Praveen as pastor, even though he was Indo-Fijian as was the vast majority of the church, and despite it all, initially he was not well received.

This lack of initial support had nothing to do with Praveen's upbringing. But within the cultural differences between native Fijians and the Indo-Fijians, there remains an intrinsic hierarchical order to the traditions of Fiji. Praveen was appointed as the pastor and, reluctantly or not, the position afforded a certain respect of and submission to his authority by those within the church. And so it was that Praveen began to lead his congregation toward calmer waters.

"Why Do You Sit Alone...?"

From the moment he assumed his position, Praveen led by example, but at first, he led with a very authoritarian style. In his mind, he was responsible for everything, not only the shepherding of the flock, but in every detail of church operations. He personally oversaw the return of his church as a source of pride within the community and a beacon of light and hope for a holy God. The people soon conceded that Praveen had honest and noble intentions. He was a good guy, but they were still wary of his heavy-handed leadership style.

Then, a few years ago, someone that our staff knew and had an established relationship with in Fiji invited Praveen to attend one of our DiscipleShift prep meetings with a small number of local pastors. These pre-conference meetings serve as a little introduction to Jesus's model of relational discipleship, to see if there is interest among key church leaders within the community and what steps we can walk out with them in their pursuit of relational discipleship.

There was one day just prior to this meeting that really stands out to me.

Praveen had recently returned from a speaking engagement in New Zealand. Our coach for the Australia/New Zealand area had been friends with Praveen for some time, and I had talked with him by phone on a few occasions and developed a good rapport with him. There were five of us in our group, and two of us got together with Praveen and his family on this particular day.

The first thing we all noticed was how unhealthy Praveen looked. His face was haggard; he was overweight and, at the time, he suffered from more than a few internal issues—all caused by stress, overwork, and overeating. He confided in us that the doctors in New Zealand had told him he probably would not live much longer if he didn't change his life habits, though he also felt that the Lord was saying he would not die because he still had work to do within his ministry. Soon after, he began the first steps on his journey back to a healthy lifestyle, physically, mentally, and spiritually.

At the meeting, Praveen was very interested in the principles of relational discipleship, and we were encouraged to return and begin working with him, which we readily agreed to do, but the key families of his church were still not tremendously on board.

Many long-standing church systems say, "We do church this way" and "We do missions that way"; although they don't necessarily have bad goals, they also don't bother to build relationships and assess where people are at—their staff, their congregation, or the community in general. How then do they know what stand to place their target on in order to hit the bull's-eye of reaching these people on a personal, relational basis? If the coaches on our missions team didn't have the relationship they had with Praveen, no one would have known what direction to go in reaching out to bridge that gap between him and his staff, not to mention the foundation of what was truly ailing him.

This is the crossroads we saw Praveen and his key leaders at: Praveen was shouldering the entire load of his church, and the people would defer to him for all of the church's decisions and direction. The leadership team, including Praveen, was not working together as one, pulling in the same direction as a cohesive unit for the good of the church.

Praveen was wearing himself out, and he was on the verge of becoming gravely ill because of the stress and pressure of his role as leader. But, in his mind, what could he do? This authoritarian style, and the sole, personal responsibility of his flock, was the only model of leadership he had ever seen.

This tug of single-minded control is something I understand very well. For many years, this was also my own leadership style. I felt personally responsible for every aspect of our budding outreach ministry, True Light Ministries. Even though I could grasp the benefit of intentional relationship, and I believed in the Scriptural basis and truthful principles of discipleship, I understood these things long before I actually began to live them out within my own life and family. And though for years Praveen had heard and understood the Biblical truths of what we were coaching him on, his leadership style had not changed.

Assessing where Praveen and his team were at by getting into relationship with them, by Praveen sharing what he shared and by us knowing him for a few years, lets us know where he and his team are at, professionally and relationally. This is how we know where to set the stand and properly place our target, and in doing so, we can take all of this information to the Lord in prayer, and ask Him to reveal where we need to illustrate Biblical truths and the direction we need to take them, from Bible Scripture.

So with that in mind, we met once again with Praveen, his staff, and some of these key families, and we went through the Biblical story of Exodus 18.

Many of you are familiar with the story. Moses had just won a huge, pivotal battle against the Amalekites, and now Jethro, his father-in-law, was coming to meet him, bringing along Moses's wife and family. Jethro's caravan arrived outside of Median, where Moses soon after arrived to greet Jethro, bowing down and kissing him. It is evident from the Scriptures that there was the utmost respect on both sides between the two men, and that day there was a great celebration and reunion between the families, and with all the people of Israel. Then, the next day:

> ...Moses sat to judge the people, and the people stood around Moses from morning till evening. When Moses' father-in-law saw all that he was doing for the people, he said, "What is this that you are doing for the people? Why do you sit alone, and all the people stand around you from morning till evening?" And Moses said to his father-in-law, "Because the people come to me to inquire of God; when they have a dispute, they come to me and I decide between one person and another, and I make them know the statutes of God and his laws." Moses' father-in-law said to him, "What you are doing is not good. You and the people with you will certainly wear yourselves out, for the thing is too heavy for you. You are not able to do it

alone. Now obey my voice; I will give you advice, and God be with you! You shall represent the people before God and bring their cases to God, and you shall warn them about the statutes and the laws, and make them know the way in which they must walk and what they must do. Moreover, look for able men from all the people, men who fear God, who are trustworthy and hate a bribe, and place such men over the people as chiefs of thousands, of hundreds, of fifties, and of tens. And let them judge the people at all times. Every great matter they shall bring to you, but any small matter they shall decide themselves. So it will be easier for you, and they will bear the burden with you. If you do this, God will direct you, you will be able to endure, and all these people will go to their place in peace. — Exodus 18:13–23, ESV

By the end of the Biblical account, Moses understood the common sense and wisdom that came from God in what Jethro suggested, and with Moses, as with Praveen, there was a willingness to let go of the iron grip of total control.

But Jethro also instructed Moses on just who he should let go his control to: "to able men who fear God, who are trustworthy and hate a bribe." Under this instruction, Moses knew the people well enough to know the individual men he could trust. Even the night that we recounted this story with him and his staff, Praveen confided that he hadn't fully trusted in his key leaders, but he was willing to begin.

Boldly, we asked the team what their part in this new understanding should be. How is Praveen able to trust unless they, as one, have shown that they were able and trustworthy, that they had an abiding faith in God as outlined in Exodus 18, and that they had an understanding of Scripture and were willing to work within Jesus's model of relationship? How might they be able to show Praveen that he can honestly and truthfully trust them? And what did they see as their part in growing as leaders?

In part, the team expressed that they truly did love Praveen and wanted to be there for him, and to tear down any walls that had been built up.

We also asked Praveen, "What would it actually look like if you increased your trust and investment into these key leaders, pouring into them, equipping them, and releasing them to assume some of the responsibility of your church duties?" In essence, what would it look like to have the team, the key leaders and families of his church, help Praveen lead? Within these questions, we also talked about the only real way in equipping and investing in one another was through relationship, and specifically by Praveen modeling what it is like to be a disciple of Jesus who makes disciples.

As a result, Praveen and his leadership began to work together, and a real transformation began to take place. It took a load off Praveen's shoulders because he began to disciple, equip, and trust these people. And his leaders began to become more excited to develop into a cohesive team, and to see God work through them as they forged ahead as one. They began ministering to those around them and formed small groups, becoming more actively involved not only in the church culture but in the lives of their families and friends, through intentional relationship.

On a personal level, Praveen began to completely change his diet and reorganize his schedule. This health crisis gave him the wakeup call he needed to instill the Biblically based knowledge and courage to make some key lifestyle changes in his life—beginning with being the husband, father, pastor, and leader he needed to be.

Today, Praveen and his staff are one of the strongest groups I've seen in terms of caring for each other, growing as disciples, having each other's backs, and taking on responsibility.

This transformation required Praveen to be transparent, vulnerable, and "real" with his team, which is, as we've seen in some of the other cultures we've discussed so far, something that is counter to the culture of Fiji, to the societal norms and expectations of the people there and, to be totally honest, at odds with the world culture in general.

This is something that we hear in most any culture we talk with: "I can't really be open and honest with anybody or they may stab me in the back." Or, "We just can't do that in this culture." Or, "Men don't do that." It's a default human nature characteristic; people like to say it is cultural, but in reality this is a hard truth of humanity that we constantly battle, both within ourselves and within the context of culture and continent, all the time. However, it has been my personal experience that 100 percent of the time Jesus's model of relational discipleship works in every single culture.

Overall, the biggest hurdle Praveen and his leadership had to overcome was the lack of openness, transparency, and relationship, and the willingness, especially on Praveen's side, to let down their guard and begin a personal, abiding connection with each other.

In many ways, Praveen's leaders—when they understood that he was trustworthy—were crying out for him to trust them, saying, in essence, "We've been here through thick and thin, and we see you are a good, God-fearing man." They were more ready to trust in the process and begin the relational process than Praveen himself.

How about you? Could the stumbling block in establishing and nurturing intentional relationship within your church and community...be you?

Disciples Unleashed

Bible verses to consider

Exodus 18 – all

John 13:1-17

Exodus 17:8-16

Matthew 20:25-28

John 14:12

Study questions for further discussion

*What did it cost Pastor Praveen to make those changes in his relationships?

*What would it cost you, and would it be worth it? What stands in your way of counting those costs?

*What do you learn from the story of Moses and Jethro that you could apply to your own life and relationships?

Chapter 7
Truly Making a Disciple of Jesus (Who Makes Disciples)

What Does It Look Like, Biblically, to Make a Disciple?

In Chapter 5 I talked about what it looks like to create a church culture based on relational discipleship, a culture that many people know as an example of the early church culture which, in reality, was the Body of Christ that Jesus had in mind all along.

It was truly a lifestyle for the followers of Christ. The believers in Acts lived out on a day-to-day basis what they had been taught and shown by the Lord's apostles.

> *They devoted themselves to the apostles' teaching and to fellowship...and had everything in common. They sold property and possessions to give to anyone who had nee...[and] continued to meet together in the temple courts. They broke bread in their homes and ate together with glad and sincere hearts, praising God...* — Acts 2:42–47, NIV (edited)

And again, as was stated in an earlier chapter, this culture is emphasized at the conclusion of Acts 4.

> *All the believers were one in heart and mind. No one claimed that any of their possessions was their own, but they shared everything they had. With great power the apostles continued to testify to the resurrection of the Lord Jesus. And God's grace was so powerfully at work in them all that there were no needy persons among them. For from time to time those who owned land or houses sold them, brought the money from the sales and put it at the apostles' feet, and it was distributed to anyone who had need.* — Acts 4:32–35, NIV

In fact, in the next verses we are given an example of what this culture looks like in the life of one such believer—a believer whose name is scattered only sparsely throughout the New Testament but who, without him, we may not have the majority of what we read in those books. His name is Joseph, but we know him better as Barnabas, and there is strong Biblical evidence that he is the man who discipled the Apostle Paul.

> *Joseph, a Levite from Cyprus, whom the apostles called Barnabas (which means "son of encouragement"), sold a field he owned and brought the money and put it at the apostles' feet.* — Acts 4:36–37, NIV

This is a very inauspicious introduction, but even so we are still able to learn a fair amount about this early companion to Paul. Barnabas was a Levite, the tribe God commissioned to be the temple priests. He was apparently well off—or had enough money or property that he could sell some, at least. And, he was selfless and generous enough to have "brought the money and put it at the apostles' feet."

Barnabas obviously had a relationship with the apostles and, possibly through this one act, garnered a certain amount of favor and influence with them. This influence is apparent five chapters later as Paul comes to Jerusalem for the first time after preaching in Damascus following his conversion and healing.

> *When he came to Jerusalem, he tried to join the disciples, but they were all afraid of him, not believing that he really was a disciple.* **But Barnabas took him and brought him to the apostles. He told them how Saul on his journey had seen the Lord and that the Lord had spoken to him, and how in Damascus he had preached fearlessly in the name of Jesus.** *So Saul stayed with them and moved about freely in Jerusalem, speaking boldly in the name of the Lord. He talked and*

> *debated with the Hellenistic Jews, but they tried to kill him. When the believers learned of this, they took him down to Caesarea and sent him off to Tarsus.* — Acts 9:26–30, NIV (emphasis mine)

Soon after, Barnabas was sent to Antioch, one of the outlying communities of believers after the scattering of the faithful following Stephen's death.

> *When [Barnabas] arrived and saw what the grace of God had done, he was glad and encouraged them all to remain true to the Lord with all their hearts. He was a good man, full of the Holy Spirit and faith, and a great number of people were brought to the Lord. Then Barnabas went to Tarsus to look for Saul, and when he found him, he brought him to Antioch. So for a whole year Barnabas and Saul met with the church and taught great numbers of people. The disciples were called Christians first at Antioch.* — Acts 11:23–26, NIV

One of the things you will notice is that in these earliest stories of the two, Barnabas is always listed first. Among Hebrew culture and writings, this is a sign of respect. Clearly, Barnabas is the early church "leader" of the two men.

By Acts chapter 13, however, there is a shift. First, the men are "set apart" (vs. 2), then they are sent on their first missionary journey (vs. 4). Saul is first called by his gentile name Paul beginning in verse 9, and then Paul's is listed first, an obvious shift in "leadership" from verses 13 on.

What happened on a day-by-day basis between these two men during this time is a mystery, but one thing is clear—Barnabas was Paul's first friend, mentor, and discipler following his conversion on the Damascus Road. And, despite a later dissension and division, his influence on the apostle cannot be overstated. Barnabas was the first (and possibly only) man to support Paul when all the others feared him; he was the one who found Paul in Tarsus and brought him into a missionary role, walking with him each step of the way and then releasing him on his first missionary journey.

So, what does it look like, Biblically, to make a disciple?

Barnabas was the man who found Paul, recognizing his interest and enthusiasm in spreading the Gospel of Christ. He was the one who brought Paul into a position of relationship and intentional teaching. He walked with him, both physically and relationally, as he mentored the apostle. And finally, he released him to begin his own ministry of evangelism and relational discipleship.

This brings us to the seventh ring of our target: personally making disciples of Jesus who make more disciples of Jesus.

So, What Does It Look Like Today to Make a Disciple?

When my wife and I were doing mission work in Mexico, our base of operation was in the city of Rosarito. During this time we became acquainted with a pastor there named Juan, who had been raised up by someone investing time into his life through intentional relationship. Juan's church was called Torre Fuerte, or "Strong Tower," and every year through our missionary work we brought people down to help meet the needs of Juan and his church family—extending the building, erecting a new bathroom, building homes for families attending their church but living in caves, and other outreaches into the neighborhood.

Each time we were there, Juan would invite us to come and meet with his senior pastor, who lived in a city about two hours away; he was the man who had spent so much time discipling Juan. But each time, scheduling and distance never afforded us the opportunity.

Then, after several years of invitation, I was able to spend most of a summer down with Juan and his team, and once again he invited me to come and meet this man. So, we all piled into a rented Ford Pinto station wagon—Juan and his family, and me and three of my interns, eleven in all—and drove to Tecate.

The trip went like you would expect it to with eleven people in a Pinto station wagon, including hitting a huge pothole at one point and breaking an axle. But eventually we arrived and met Juan's mentor. His name was Ariel Romero, and it was a meeting that would change my life.

Pastor Ariel and Pastor Oscar

Pastor Ariel Romero is the founder and president of Ministerio Vino y Aceite, or Ministry of Wine and Oil (a name taken from the parable of the good Samaritan), in Tecate, Mexico. He was raised in a family of Christian believers, and his parents also have a strong background in business.

Ariel felt a call into the ministry starting at a young age and, upon graduating from high school, he began studies at a Bible college in Ensenada. During his time at the college, he felt a prompting from the Holy Spirit that his role was to go and plant a church. Of course, his assumption was that he would go and fulfill this calling after his graduation from Bible college, but the prompting remained insistent.

Then, one day while he was returning from a visit to his family in Tecate, he was driving back to the college in Ensenada when, once more, he felt the strong prompting of the Lord to start his church. In his words, the Lord wanted him to do it "now"!

"So I looked," he said, "and there was enough gas in the tank to make it to Rosarito. So that is where I went, right then, and planted my first church."

Despite his relatively young age, it was a successful church plant. His congregation was, on average, of a fairly young age, and Ariel's infectious enthusiasm for the Word brought people into the church.

After two or three years of leading his people, the prompting to plant a church returned. By this time, Ariel had a firm grasp of the concepts of relational discipleship; he had raised up a few key leaders, and he felt comfortable in leaving the church in the hands of one of the men he had discipled while he answered the Lord's calling.

Once again he followed the concepts of relationship that had worked well for him in Rosarito, and he repeated the process again and again until after a few years he had successfully planted four or five new churches.

Up until this point, Ariel had always been the one who had raised up his successor, then left and planted another church. But after this he began to change his approach. He saw in the Bible the concept of a multiplication of disciples instead of merely addition. When Ariel raised men up and then stepped out to plant another church, he was adding up disciples one at a time. Now, he began to raise up disciples who he could then send out to be church planters and pastors. Those men could then raise up their own disciples who could make disciples, and so on—in other words, multiplying his numbers exponentially instead of simply adding them by ones.

During our first meeting together, Ariel cast a vision to me of what the Lord had put on his heart, which was to establish 1,000 churches in Mexico. He called them "ports of entry into God's kingdom," saying, "There needs to be a port of entry into God's kingdom in every city."

At that point, when I met him, there were seven.

That was fourteen years ago.

Ariel took me around to some of those churches he had planted in the Tecate area. It was one of the times in my life when I heard the Lord's strong prompting within my own heart. Our ministry in Mexico, True Light Ministries, was growing, and for years we had always been based out of Rosarito. But what I heard from the Lord was that, whatever we do down in Mexico, we needed to come alongside this man, Ariel.

So the following year, we actually shifted our base from Rosarito to Tecate. It seemed foolhardy from a "logical" standpoint, and we knew it, but the prompting of the Holy Spirit would not be denied. We had no place to stay. We had no tools. Yet we still were able to bring down several teams throughout that first summer, staying in a man's home who later became a pastor for one of Ariel's church plants.

It was a small home, and there were twenty-three of us! We were camped out all over the floor, sleeping in sleeping bags and stepping over each other no matter where we wanted to go.

Truly Making a Disciple of Jesus (Who Makes Disciples)

Our task that first summer was to build a church. I had never built anything bigger than a 24 x 24 house, and before that, my biggest building was a shed.

Our first task in the first week was to build outhouses, because the second week we were bringing a team of over fifty down. Our goal was that we were going to live and eat and sleep in the church structure as we were building it—roof or no roof. And, yes, it rained. Thank God for tarps!

We designed this church using scrawled-out sketches on napkins as our blueprints, ending up with a 2,000 square foot building which is still standing today, thirteen years later! (I'm sure this is due much more to the powerful blessing of God's Spirit than to any of our meager construction abilities.)

The pastor we built this church for was a man named Oscar Escebedo.

Oscar was a man who Ariel had been working with for a few years, identifying him early on as a disciple who was faithful, hungry for the Word, and humble yet confident enough to be sent out.

Like Barnabas with Paul, and then Paul later on with Timothy, Ariel began investing his time and energies with Oscar, basically doing life with him—preaching, teaching, visiting people in their homes or in the hospital, having meetings. Wherever Ariel went, he took Oscar with him.

Oscar was a brand-new pastor when we finally prayed over that church we had built and then handed him the keys. Prior to that, he and his congregation had been meeting either outdoors or in people's homes, but the sheer numbers of people were making this a rather difficult task to continue.

Through it all, Ariel maintained his close relationship with Oscar, even after releasing him and though they were now responsible for two different church bodies.

> *He is the one we proclaim, admonishing and teaching everyone with all wisdom, so that we may present everyone fully mature in Christ.* — Colossians 1:28, NIV

Fast-forward many years, and Ariel's network of churches has grown to between eighty to ninety in number. Ariel is still based in Tecate, where he oversees Ministerio Vino y Aceite, the discipleship ministry he founded to bring in key leaders together, identified through the communities where there is a desire for a church plant, in order to teach them, disciple them, and most importantly, grow in relationship with them in order to release them into the community to begin their own ministry and discipleship process.

Today, Ariel's ministry influence has been extended to the point where he is being invited to other nations—Nicaragua, Honduras, and other Central American countries—to speak and to plant churches. As this opportunity for worldwide outreach arose, Ariel found that he needed to bring someone in to take over the ministry within Mexico.

Who do you suppose he chose?

Oscar Escebedo, of course.

Timothy, my dear son, be strong through the grace that God gives you in Christ Jesus. You have heard me teach things that have been confirmed by many reliable witnesses. Now teach these truths to other trustworthy people who will be able to pass them on to others...Teach these things and insist that everyone learn them. Don't let anyone think less of you because you are young. Be an example to all believers... — 2 Timothy 2:1–2, 1 Timothy 4:11–12, NLT

It is not that common for leaders to release portions of their ministry "well." Some are reluctant to let go, some hold on with an iron grip, and some do not do enough in equipping their successors, if anything at all. There are many potholes along the road to success where a mentor can "break an axle." Even our Biblical examples of Paul and Barnabas had their rocky relations at times.

But raising up disciples who make disciples is the key factor within the model and plan that Jesus has showed us. It is not enough that we preach the Word. We need to live it out, intentionally, and teach others to do the same. In this way we can allow the influence of the Holy Spirit to increase exponentially (one that can generate countless thousands of potential results), rather than by addition (one to the next, to the next, individually).

Ariel continues to be Oscar's spiritual father, authority, and counselor, just as Paul was to Timothy and, like a proud father, Ariel says that Oscar is "doing even more than when I was leading our ministry in Mexico."

Oscar continues on in the tradition and example set down for him and is following in Ariel's footsteps, raising up key leaders in relational discipleship, planting more churches in the Tecate area, and replacing himself as pastor within his original church.

This is the model of Jesus, of the apostles, of Barnabas, and of Paul. It should just as well be ours who also claim His name.

Disciple-Makers Making Disciple-Makers

DiscipleShift is an intensive two-day gathering of pastors and church leaders that focuses on creating a reproducible process of Biblical, relational discipleship, and there is a lot of information that is crammed into those two days. A lot! In fact, I am often asked, "How much of the discipleship process do people who come to DiscipleShift actually retain?"

That's a good question. The problem is, it isn't the right question. It's not about how much head knowledge a person walks away with; it's about the heart change that takes place on a spiritual level, and here's what I mean.

What happens during a DiscipleShift event is that we try to share the information we've been able to glean on Biblical, relational discipleship. And again, it is a lot of information.

During those two days of DiscipleShift, I believe the Lord touches people's hearts at different times. Wherever the people are at in their spiritual walk, God is willing to give as much as each person is willing to receive. It's a heart change through the Spirit's prompting. God unveils the Scriptural truth behind the model, and this mode of connection is a beneficial tool for both congregational growth and a deeper, abiding relationship with family, friends, staff, and others.

But, realistically, most people will only "get" about 20 to 30 percent of the information we offer. And then, they will take what material they've gathered back and share it with their people. I compare it to opening a fire hydrant of knowledge and the people who attend are able to walk away with their own bucketful of knowledge—a large bucket, but only a bucket. And, of what they share with their teams, those folks are able to walk away with merely a cupful of that knowledge.

That wouldn't be good if that were the end of the whole process. But building relationships, and fostering relational environments, is not a one-and-done process. It's a journey. It's a marathon. Intentional, relational discipleship is not something you teach. It is something you live. It is something that just becomes a part of what you do and who you are.

Through these ongoing, intentional relationships, with God and with other disciples, your bucket continues to get filled. And as a result, you are able to pass on cupful after cupful to your friends, family, coworkers, and key leaders, who then pass out their thimblefuls as well. Before long, you find out that your bucket has become a fire hydrant, and the cups have become buckets, and on it goes. Like we say: It becomes a case of multiplication instead of addition.

If the thought of this process discourages you in any way, just think of Jesus and His original twelve apostles. These men were with Him for over three years and yet were able to comprehend only a small fraction of what He was teaching. They continually missed the point or questioned Him, or even doubted, right up to Peter's denial and Thomas's refusal to believe until he put his hand on Jesus's side and in His hands. But...

After the resurrection, the eleven who remained understood a great deal more! And yet their journey still hadn't ended there. They continued their growth, passing it on to others—to the church in Acts, to Barnabas and Paul, to John Mark and Timothy, all the way to us today.

Yes, we can count ourselves among the multiplication of the discipleship process begun by the apostles over two thousand years ago! And the beauty is that we now get to pass on our thimbleful to the next generation of believers—almost as if God had designed it that way all along!

In this whole explosion of living out Jesus's plan for discipleship, an amazing aha moment occurs when those within the discipleship process begin to understand the Biblical model and say, "Yeah, we want to go in that direction!" Creating this abiding relational culture within a church is a necessity for any kind of sustainable church development, and for a deepening sense of spiritual growth.

But a true mark in the realization of "fruit" from the efforts of disciple making is when you are able to make this model of discipleship reproducible: disciples who make disciples who make disciples, a perpetual state of multiplication instead of addition.

Brother F

> ...*even as I try to please everyone in every way. For I am not seeking my own good but the good of many, so that they may be saved. Follow my example, as I follow the example of Christ.* — 1 Corinthians 10:33–11:1, ESV

Brother F is a pastor overseeing a large ministry operation in one of the more destitute southeast countries of Asia. He is also one of the smartest guys I know. His life is at risk on a daily basis because of where he has chosen to take the Gospel. There is a militant religious compound, hostile to Christians, just a few miles from one of his ministries, and similar groups have shot up his house. His brother-in-law has been kidnapped and held, the people telling him to change what he is doing (in spreading the Gospel), or he and his family would be killed. They have since fled to a nearby country, seeking political asylum. But Brother F and his family remain, and he is a much higher profile, outspoken proponent of Christ than they were.

Brother F's attitude is similar to Peter and John in Acts 4.

> *Then [the Sanhedrin] called them in again and commanded them not to speak or teach at all in the name of Jesus. But Peter and John replied, "Which is right in God's eyes: to listen to you, or to him? You be the judges! As for us, we cannot help speaking about what we have seen and heard."*
>
> *After further threats they let them go. They could not decide how to punish them, because all the people were praising God for what had happened.* — Acts 4:18–21, NIV

> And again in Acts 5:40–42 — *"...They called the apostles in and had them flogged. Then they ordered them not to speak in the name of Jesus, and let them go. The apostles left the Sanhedrin, rejoicing because they had been counted worthy of suffering disgrace for the Name. Day after day, in the temple courts and from house to house, they never stopped teaching and proclaiming the good news that Jesus is the Messiah.*

These passages personify how Brother F lives. He has told me, "If they kill me, they kill me, and I am at peace with that. And, if they kill my wife or my kids, I am at peace with that as well." Honestly, I don't know if my own faith runs that deep, and I pray never to have it tested in such a way as this. If we choose to make a stand for Jesus here in America, we may lose some friends or maybe even a job, but our life, and the lives of our family, those threats that Brother F lives with on a daily basis, is not something we really even contemplate here in America. But this reality makes the cost of being a disciple of Jesus Christ that much clearer in some of these more militantly religious countries.

When we first began a relationship with him, one of the first things we saw in Brother F was his level of excitement at being able to implement the discipleship process within his own country. For years he has had teams of ministries and churches behind him in both the United States and abroad, supporting him prayerfully, Scripturally, and financially, and great things were happening within his ministry. Schools were being built, pastors were being supported, people were coming to know the Lord, and the fruits of his labor were being harvested day after day. In fact, one of the unique areas of support, and one of Brother F's most effective tools of ministry and outreach, was in supplying portable recording devices—MP3 players, iPods, and the like. On these small devices, Biblical books and Gospel stories could be recorded in the people's own native languages and played during small group meetings or at work camps where laborers toil for ten to twelve hours each day, seven days a week, to make bricks or other hard labor.

> *...what you have heard from me...entrust to faithful men who will be able to teach others also...*

But then, when Brother F first learned of Jesus's model of relational discipleship, he was immediately on board and instantly began implementing the process within his own leadership team. His key leaders were equally as enthusiastic, and the result was in the growth of his team from six or seven leaders and seventy villages to around fourteen leaders and over two hundred villages in a relatively short amount of time.

Like the fire hydrant and bucket comparison, out of everything we shared with him, Brother F most readily understood the concept of and need for small groups. This type of relational coming together of the congregation was something he and his leadership had not done before. Oh, they were meeting in people's houses, moving from place to place, with a relatively small numbers of congregants, but it was still very much expository preaching—being told the word or having it read to them, very one directional, instead of each person living it out with their own homes and families on a daily basis.

The concept of intentional relationship within the small group setting had tremendous impact, and the people embraced it immediately; soon they began meeting every day. At the time, we told them that we were not mandating they would need to meet every single day as a requirement of discipleship. But most often the people responded with, "Other than this we have nothing. This gives us a reason for life beyond the hours and days spent working in the labor camps. We actually look forward to this time."

At first, these groups continued in the mold of Bible study or Bible listening, with one person leading. But we continued to feed in to Brother F's "bucket," coaching and mentoring him and his staff, continually coming alongside these teams and their leaders. Through this ongoing connection, we were able to convey more of the concept of "relationship" into the small group mix. The people were able to see the importance of investing time into each other's lives, and that each person could have input into the discussion about God's Word; they could ask questions, give opinions, hash out understandings, and so on.

With the unfolding of this new relational model, the leadership was able to travel from town to town and meet with each group once a week or once every two weeks, and soon it became necessary to train up people under each leader, an apprentice within each respective group, someone able to live out the discipleship model within each of the towns, and groups, and families where they were meeting. In other words, they were beginning to multiply.

The pastors were also learning to facilitate and not simply preach; they asked questions, got to know the people, and encouraged them to discuss Scripture passages among themselves, discipling the people on how to personally apply God's Word into their own lives. For those within this repressed culture, gathered together in these small group settings, it was revolutionary. Just think of it, the people were allowed to speak as much, or even more so, than their leaders, including the women—something unheard of prior to this in their culture.

As the "bucket" of Brother F began to grow, so too did the "buckets" of his staff and leadership; soon, the pastors began to understand the reproducible concept of relational discipleship—that what Brother F had passed on to them, they were able to pass on to each of their respective small groups. And those leaders could, in turn, invest in someone else within the group, raising up future leaders as the group would grow and branch.

In places like this South Asia country where Brother F calls home, this model works. It works even under such stringent persecution. It works because it is Jesus's model.

As I said at the beginning, Brother F's life is on the line every day because of where he has chosen to take the Gospel, and he has come to embrace the mindset that if he dies, he dies, and if he lives, he lives, and may he be praising God in either situation. The people he works with and ministers to, and the people he lives with day to day in intentional relationship, living out Jesus's model of discipleship with each other and with their families, embrace this mindset as well.

God bless them in their faith and on their journey.

Bible verses to consider

Acts 2:42-47

Acts 4:32-37

Acts 9:26-30

Acts 11:23-26

Colossians 1:28

2 Timothy 2:1-2

1 Timothy 4:11-12

1 Cor. 10:33-11:1

Acts 4:18-21

Matthew 28:18-20

Matthew 22:34-40

Study questions for further discussion

*How is the continuing multiplication of disciples a key part of Jesus's plan?

*What characteristics of Pastor Ariel cause him to be a man who makes disciples of Jesus who make more disciples?

*What do the answers to the first two questions teach you about yourself?

Chapter 8
It Starts with the "Be"

The Apostle Peter has always been a great inspiration for me, mostly because he was just so human.

I think we, as Christians, want to believe that our heroes of the Bible are these perfect examples of how to act, how to believe, how to have faith to move mountains, and what the ideal God-fearing man or woman should look like. But in reality, most everyone you read of in Scripture is just as flawed, doubtful, weak, and human as you or me. And that's a good thing. Moses, for instance, had a speaking problem; David was an adulterer and murderer; Gideon was a coward; and Paul had a "thorn in his flesh" (whether physical, emotional, or addictive) that, even through fervent prayer, the Lord did not remove from him, and Peter...

Peter was an impulsive, headstrong fisherman—a kind of "leap before you look" type of guy. He does amazing things for the Lord, he has tremendous insight, he displays incredible faith...and then he messes up, sometimes just a few moments later.

> *When Jesus came to the region of Caesarea Philippi, he asked his disciples, "Who do people say the Son of Man is?" They replied, "Some say John the Baptist; others say Elijah; and still others, Jeremiah or one of the prophets."*
>
> *"But what about you?" he asked. "Who do you say I am?"*
>
> *Simon Peter answered, "You are the Messiah, the Son of the living God."*
>
> *Jesus replied, "Blessed are you, Simon son of Jonah, for this was not revealed to you by flesh and blood, but by my Father in heaven. And I tell you that you are Peter, and on this rock I will build my church, and the gates of Hades will not overcome it...From that time on Jesus began to explain to his disciples that he*

> *must go to Jerusalem and suffer many things at the hands of the elders, the chief priests and the teachers of the law, and that he must be killed and on the third day be raised to life. Peter took him aside and began to rebuke him. "Never, Lord!" he said. "This shall never happen to you!"*
>
> *Jesus turned and said to Peter, "Get behind me, Satan! You are a stumbling block to me; you do not have in mind the concerns of God, but merely human concerns."* — Matthew 16:13–18, 21–23, NIV

See? Tremendous insight in one moment and, in the next, Jesus needs to take him aside and say, "Look, dude, you have no idea what you're talking about." (I'm paraphrasing a little.)

Just imagine the faith it took Peter to step out of the boat during a raging storm...but then he takes his eyes off Jesus, the very source of his faith, suddenly realizing where that faith had taken him, and he begins to sink. Peter is the one who rushes to the Messiah's aid in the garden, sword in hand...only to be told that "those who draw the sword will die by the sword." Peter swears he will never deny Jesus...then after the Lord is taken away, he does just that. Three times!

In other words he's a lot like us—or a lot like me, anyway—and yet through it all, Jesus is with him every step of the way, continually restoring and teaching him.

Discipling him.

Which leads us to the final ring in our target—one that's at the very center, and the one that also affects every ring that radiates out from here.

The Bull's-Eye: Personally Being a Disciple of Jesus

In his heart, even during the first time that Peter met the Lord, he understands almost immediately who Jesus is, and who (and what) he is within himself before such an overwhelming presence of power and grace:

> *On one occasion, while the crowd was pressing in on him to hear the word of God, he was standing by the lake of Gennesaret [that is, the Sea of Galilee], and he saw two boats by the lake, but the fishermen had gone out of them and were washing their nets. Getting into one of the boats, which was Simon's, he asked him to put out a little from the land. And he sat down and taught the people from the boat. And when he had finished speaking, he said to Simon, "Put out into the deep and let down your nets for a catch." And Simon answered, "Master, we toiled all night and took nothing! But at your word I will let down the nets." And when they had done this, they enclosed a large number of fish, and their nets were breaking. They signaled to their partners in the other boat to come and help them. And they came and filled both the boats, so that they began to sink.* **But when Simon Peter saw it, he fell down at Jesus' knees, saying, "Depart from me, for I am a sinful man, O Lord." For he and all who were with him were astonished at the catch of fish that they had taken,** *and so also were James and John, sons of Zebedee, who were partners with Simon. And Jesus said to Simon, "Do not be afraid; from now on you will be catching men." And when they had brought their boats to land, they left everything and followed him.* — Luke 5:1–11, ESV

(emphasis mine)

As I said before, Peter is a very zealous and enthusiastic man, but his impulsiveness is kind of all over the map. His heart is always in the right place, but his ambition sometimes gets the best of him. Even so, as a disciple he is always growing.

The man who denied his association with the Christ three times is the same man, forty or so days later, in Acts 2, who we see becoming this passionate, courageous, and dynamic speaker. Thousands have assembled on the day of Pentecost below the window where the apostles have been in seclusion, when God sends His Holy Spirit to begin a revolution, and up steps Peter, more mature in his walk yet still very much human, boldly proclaiming the resurrection and living presence of the Messiah.

In fact, just before this moment, there is this small exchange between Christ and Peter, following the resurrection, which shows Peter in all of his ambition and humanity. Jesus has just appeared to several of the apostles on the shore of the Sea of Galilee, and Jesus asks Peter three different times the same question, "Do you love me?"

> *Peter was hurt because Jesus asked him the third time, "Do you love me?" He said, "Lord, you know all things; you know that I love you."*
>
> *Jesus said, "Feed my sheep. Very truly I tell you, when you were younger you dressed yourself and went where you wanted; but when you are old you will stretch out your hands, and someone else will dress you and lead you where you do not want to go." Jesus said this to indicate the kind of death by which Peter would glorify God. Then he said to him, "Follow me!"*
>
> *Peter turned and saw that the disciple whom Jesus loved was following them...When Peter saw him, he asked, "Lord, what about him?"*
>
> *Jesus answered, "If I want him to remain alive until I return, what is that to you? You must follow me."* — John 21:17b–22, NIV

I love that! Jesus has just revealed to Peter how he will die, and glorify God in the process, and Peter's first question?

"What about him?" (Meaning John, the "disciple Jesus loved.")

It Starts With the "Be"

And isn't that a lot like how we are? How many times have I dealt with a tragedy, or overcome some obstacle in my life, even to look back and see how God worked all of it out for my ultimate good, and for His glory, only to then turn back around and ask, "But what about them, God? Why aren't they going through trials, too? Why do they have it so good? Why do I have to struggle so much?"?

Sure, I find a lot of comfort in knowing that many of the answers I seek can be found in the Bible. I also find just as much comfort that, even when I can't find the answers, I can usually find someone within the Bible who has asked the same questions, struggled with the same issues, or faced the same doubts as I have.

You see, not all of our questions have answers, at least not at the time we're looking for them, and maybe not for a good while after. And that too is a good thing, as long as it keeps us searching, keeps us learning, and keeps us discovering. Peter is a real-life example that we do not have to be perfect. We don't need perfect faith, a perfect attitude, and the perfect answers in order to be a real disciple of Jesus.

Jesus allows for the ups and downs in our lives, and He even walks with us through them. If we let Him. Because here is the best part: Reaching for perfection in any of these areas is not a bad thing. But it is also not the point. Having the ability and willingness to abide in Christ through all of our ups and downs, and having the right people to walk with us along the way...

That's the point.

> *"I am the true grapevine, and my Father is the gardener. He cuts off every branch of mine that doesn't produce fruit, and he prunes[8] the branches that do bear fruit so they will produce even more. You have already been pruned and purified by the message I have*

---

[8] The Greek word used here is αἴρω, or airó, and can be translated as "raise up," "lift up," "take away," or "remove." Some translations also use the term "clean."

> *given you. Remain in me, and I will remain in you. For a branch cannot produce fruit if it is severed from the vine, and you cannot be fruitful unless you remain in me."* — John 15:1–2, NLT

As you spend time with Jesus, you may still mess up, but Jesus loves you through that, and the Holy Spirit still speaks into your life to lead you into a more perfect relationship through each misstep. There may be pruning, there may be discipline, there may be hard questions and even harder answers, but through it all, Jesus is leading us into a deeper and more intimate and abiding relationship with Himself.

> *because the Lord disciplines the one he loves,*
> *and he chastens everyone he accepts as his son.*
> *...[Our earthly fathers] disciplined us for a little while as they thought best; but God disciplines us for our good, in order that we may share in his holiness.* — Hebrews 12:6, 10, NIV

Even in our faults and failures, in our strengths and weaknesses, we are still disciples of Jesus. And if we persevere, Jesus, through our intentional relationship with the Holy Spirit, will strengthen us to finish our calling as His true disciples.

> *When they saw the courage of Peter and John and realized that they were unschooled, ordinary men, they were astonished and they took note that these men had been with Jesus.* — Acts 4:13, NIV

"Unschooled, ordinary person who had been with Jesus"—that is something I would be proud to have etched on my tombstone.

Let's talk a little more here about what it means to be a disciple of Jesus Christ and, just like when we looked at the definitions of "church" and "Christian," we need to begin with a proper definition. For that, there is no better place to go than into God's Word.

In Matthew 4:19 we see an invitation Jesus gives to Peter and Andrew, and to us, to become His disciples. He says, "Come, follow me, and I will make you fishers of men."

The invitation to become Jesus's disciple starts with an invitation, "Come," and an instruction, "Follow me." A disciple has been invited into relationship and is now a follower of Christ. But not just a casual, sometimes, "kinda"-type follower, but an honest and abiding follower with a genuine, tangible relationship—loving Jesus, getting to know Jesus, learning about Jesus, learning *from* Jesus, and growing in understanding, and getting closer and closer to Jesus day by day. That is the kind of follower Jesus is inviting us to be.

Now, it's easy to skip over the next part of the invitation—"and I will make you..."—but, in many ways, this is the best, most powerful, and most important part of our personal walk. When we enter into this relationship with Jesus, when we begin to follow Him, He will make us, change us, and transform us more and more into His likeness.

> *For those God foreknew he also predestined to be conformed to the image of his Son, that he might be the firstborn among many brothers and sisters.* — Romans 8:29, NIV

This is not only good news, this is essential, because we cannot do it ourselves; we don't have the ability nor the power required to undertake such a radical life-shift on our own. Jesus, on the other hand, has more than sufficient of both. This amazing miracle, motivated by love, means that Jesus takes us as we are and literally begins a reclamation project, a complete renovation of our heart, mind, and spirit.

> *Therefore, I urge you, brothers and sisters, in view of God's mercy, to offer your*

> *bodies as a living sacrifice, holy and pleasing to God—this is your true and proper worship. Do not conform to the pattern of this world, but be transformed by the renewing of your mind. Then you will be able to test and approve what God's will is—his good, pleasing and perfect will.* — Romans 12:1–2, NIV

When you have a moment, spend some time in the verses of Ephesians 2 to gain even more understanding of what God is doing within you and the lives of your fellow believers as we choose to follow Jesus and be His disciple.

The third part of Jesus's invitation says He will make us "fishers of men." This is Jesus's desire for His church, for us, to become living and active "fishing vessels" as He transforms us into becoming more and more like Him. He allows us to be on mission with Him, to "be about [His] Father's business," just like He was, and is.

What an awesome, loving, grace-filled plan!

> *Students are not greater than their teacher. But the student who is fully trained will become like the teacher.* — Luke 6:40, NLT

> *For we are God's handiwork, created in Christ Jesus to do good works, which God prepared in advance for us to do.* — Ephesians 2:10, NIV

> *We are therefore Christ's ambassadors, as though God were making his appeal through us. We implore you on Christ's behalf: Be reconciled to God.* — 2 Corinthians 5:20, NIV

A Disciple of Jesus—A Beacon of Light in a Desperate World

Ajai Lall was born and raised in India. From the first time I met him, he struck me as a very intelligent and committed man of God, having earned a degree in criminal law from the University of Sagar with the intention of becoming a lawyer. Instead, under the guidance and influence of his father, Dr. Vijai Lall, he sensed the call from God to serve the suffering communities of his home country, which led him to become a preacher instead. Soon after, along with his wife Indu, Ajai founded Central India Christian Mission in 1982.

Ajai is one of the most humble people I know. Within India's cultural caste system, being a pastor, even a Christian pastor, means you are the "chief" of that congregation, with its inherent honor and reverence. Within the Indian culture, as a sign of submission, people will often bow to a "superior," touching the back of their knee or their ankle as a sign of respect. Ajai has been known to intercept the greeter's hand, shaking it instead and raising the man up, smiling and even calling him "brother"—in essence, declaring that they are equals in the eyes of the God that Ajai worships.

Ajai and the church ministry of Central India Christian Ministry (CICM) have planted over 1,400 churches in India and several surrounding countries so far, and more than 700,000 unreached people have received the Gospel because of the work of CICM.

Like the Apostle Peter, Ajai is a very passionate and courageous disciple of God, and his heart is in the right place. Many of us in the pastoral field would find it easy under such widespread reach. Ajai could easily say, "We are doing fine. We have 1,400 churches. We've had 65,000 baptisms in the last year. What do I possibly need to be taught to improve on all that?" Yet, on the contrary, Ajai has a willingness to learn and grow. He recognizes the need to transform his relationships, first and foremost within his family and closest advisors, in order to align himself with the teachings and example of Jesus Christ. Like the church that sprung from the confident examples of Peter and the apostles following Jesus's ascension, CICM has become a beacon of light in a desperate world, effectively reaching out to the poor in spirit as well as the poor in abundance.

> *...praising God and enjoying the favor of all the people. And the Lord added to their number daily those who were being saved.*

According to statistics compiled by CICM, India is home to the majority of the world's unreached people groups. Currently, the Christian population is only about 6 percent. In Central and North India and the surrounding countries, more than 88 percent of the people groups have never even heard the Gospel of Jesus Christ.

In India, 443 million people live on less than $1 per day. Almost half of the children suffer from malnourishment—the highest rate in the world. Every day, 5000 children under the age of five years old die from preventable diseases. Economic progress is coming to parts of India, but much of the country still suffers extreme poverty, malnutrition, disease, and illiteracy.

Through CICM, Ajai and his ministry team are able to respond to the needs of the people in central and northern India as well as three neighboring countries, and serve people through local outreach, medical care, disaster relief, and Biblical training and discipleship. Their ministries include a children's ministry and orphanage, a nursing school, five Bible colleges, and what they term "Aatma Vikas" (taken from the Hindi words for "self-progress"), which is a service provided to local communities in India through technical training centers that offer guidance and education for local leaders and villagers to become financially self-sufficient.

When I first met Ajai and began talking to him about Jesus's model of relational discipleship, he received our conversation enthusiastically, eager to implement such a model within his own ministry structure and compelled to make changes within his own personal relationships, including his marriage and family.

There are many pastors around the world who are amazing leaders, eager to grow their ministry, but many of them are not willing to live out what it means to be a disciple, the transparent honesty built through personal relationships and without which their ministries—though successful in width and numbers—risk becoming severely limited in their depth and personal attachment to each other, and to Jesus.

Ajai Lall is without a doubt an amazing man and servant of God, and with the help of his family and staff, he has built a truly amazing ministry against some of the most difficult poverty and persecution you could imagine. But even a man of his humility and willingness is not without his flawed humanity.

It was on a return trip to visit Ajai when our team met up with him and his staff to see what inroads had been made in living out Jesus's model of relational discipleship. We were surprised when several of his staff said that, though most things were going very well, there was an aspect of openness and transparency that seemed to still be missing within the relationships between Ajai and his core team. The team felt certain walls remained between the director and his staff, and they did not feel they could come and tell him anything in confidence without risk to their relationship.

Ajai, on the other hand, felt he was being open and honest, that he was willing to listen unconditionally and that he had a good rapport with his closest advisors.

And, by his definition, he did.

But as we began to revisit the Biblical model of Jesus and His disciples, Ajai was willing to hear and accept that there was still a lot of work to be done. Moses was willing to listen to the wise, God-led counsel of Jethro. Even John the Baptist said, "He must increase, but I must decrease," knowing his role was not as the leader, but as the one who pointed the way.

The staff as well admitted that there were areas that they could work on to facilitate the changes that needed to take place. We are prayerfully walking alongside our brothers and sisters at CICM, with Ajai leading the way as they follow Jesus, are changed by Jesus, and continue on mission with Jesus.

No one this side of heaven is without their flaws, troubles, blind spots, and imperfections. We all need each other, as fellow Christ-followers and disciples, to live out what intentional relationships can truly be, in an open and transparent environment. Not so we can point up each other's flaws, but so we can catch each other as we fall, so we can build each other up instead of tearing each other, and ourselves, down, and so we can be the city on a hill that Jesus calls us to be.

Biblically, the two "ships"—discipleship and relationship—are inextricably intertwined. There is no Biblical discipleship outside of relationship, and a real relationship with God and with other believers, when lived out according to Biblical definitions and model, is the perfect, God-created incubator for being and making disciples.

Bible verses to consider

Matthew 16:13-18	Philippians 1:6
Luke 5:1-11	Ephesians 2:1-10
John 21:18-22	Luke 6:40
John 15:1-2	Matthew 28:18-20
Hebrews 12:6 & 10	2 Corinthians 5:20
Acts 4:13	Matthew 4:19
Romans 8:29	

Study questions for further discussion

*What do you learn from the apostle Peter's life that can help you be a disciple of Jesus?

*Why is the bull's-eye "BE"?

*How would you apply Matthew 4:19 personally?

Chapter 9
And, It Works in All Cultures... Even Yours!

The model of intentional, relational discipleship that Jesus gave to the twelve, and to us, is a model that works in any culture. It only stands to reason that this model would work regardless of tradition and custom; Jesus was both the perfect disciple and the perfect disciple-maker, and His is the perfect model to follow and to pass on.

Jesus was very purposeful in the conversations He had with His disciples, as recorded in Scripture. He was also intentional in the opportunities He gave to them, sending them out individually, or by twos, talking to them about the difficulties they encountered and celebrating with them their successes. He did not expect perfection; otherwise, his followers would have only lasted a few miles into their journey. But despite any shortcomings, or even at times because of them, He continued to invest in them—loving them, growing them, equipping them for acts of service, and then releasing them into an oftentimes hostile world.

One part of Jesus's model that many of us struggle with today is this intentional aspect of relational discipleship. This piece requires a concerted effort, a willingness to engage, and a courageous honesty within that engagement. It's what I call a "life-on-life investment," doing more than just talking at someone or giving them a twelve-point booklet on how to be the perfect disciple, but actually talking with them, spending time in getting to know them, to know their needs, their families, their lives, in order to "speak the truth in love" into their life and to allow them to speak with that same truth into yours.

In the Christian world, we have morphed this level of depth and intentionality into more of an "informational dump" investment of time, simply teaching, lecturing, and pontificating on Scriptural truths at the expense (or avoidance) of investing our actual time into the actual lives of actual people within our actual spheres of influence—whether those spheres are work, home, family, or friends.

When we simply teach or lecture the Word to one another, we risk missing the best and most crucial part: the entire relational aspect of Jesus's model, and the reality of what's called "doing life" together. Jesus shared everything with His disciples, eating with them, fishing with them, traveling with them, talking with them, and even praying with them. Within these shared experiences, Jesus showed a level of transparency, honesty, and vulnerability with His chosen twelve, even more so with His closest three, and to a certain degree with the hundreds that followed Him along His journey.

In general, we all tend to struggle with these types of relationships, no matter the level of transparency or the sphere of influence we are in. We struggle with the almost ungraspable concept of loving one another unconditionally, to bear one another's burdens in order to carry one another through—and sometimes in spite of—our weaknesses.

This, in great part, is because most of us have a hard time showing vulnerability, of exposing our weaknesses or exuding anything other than control, resilience, and a strong spirit (regardless of whether this inability to be transparent is through our own well-crafted façade, or through the misguided expectations of a fallen world). Our fear is that anything exposed as a weakness or vulnerability can possibly be taken and used as a weapon to hurt us or our families, or to damage our reputation or position.

Though there may be a small modicum of truth to this fear, what I have seen, both here in the United States as well as around the world, is that most often this fear stems from our own misguided perceptions rather than on any sense of reality. It can be a reality in some circumstances—which is certainly a cost to be counted—but the reality is nowhere near as wide and deep as our own drummed-up possibilities that, well, it might happen! This is an internally created issue that I see so many people struggle with in all communities where I have visited and worked, and this struggle rises up regardless of any cultural or custom.

In point of fact, it has very little to do with culture.

These fears and misperceptions really speak more to basic human nature; every culture espouses this fear, thinking quite certainly that their culture is the exception.

"Well, we know you might be able to do this over there, but you can't do it here. It just won't work here."

The problem is...every culture says that.

Jesus lived with those same preconceived notions of culture. But Jesus's model worked. It worked in ancient Israel. It worked when His disciples spread both the model and message around the known world in the early church. It is working today as we follow it in Post Falls, Idaho. And I have seen it work in every single culture, and every single country, where His disciples have been courageous enough to live out His model.

Who Has the Time for This?

We were in Israel, sharing discipleship principles with pastors from throughout the region, when one of the pastors raised a couple of objections about the model of intentional relationship. His first objection came as we were discussing the concept of small groups. We were asked what a good relational number of participants might be, and we answered that ten to fifteen would be a good number, though six to eight would also be fine, and overall, twelve is a good target. The man's objection was this: "That number wouldn't work here. Who came up with that number?"

Umm, Jesus?

However his main objection came when we began to discuss the Biblical concepts of sharing our lives with one another, of getting to know each other in deeper, more meaningful ways, and of being open and transparent within those relationships. Each of these we brought out as examples of what true, Biblical discipleship can and should look like one person to another.

"That's just not something we would be able to do here," the man said, and for good measure added, "and even if we could, who has the time for this?"

This objection seemed not only to be a cultural restraint, but also a time constraint as well, and actually it's a very valid question.

This is often the hang-up of many would-be disciples in going out into the world—this idea of building relationships and making disciples among the constant tug and pull of other commitments, other jobs, of family obligations and everything else that all of us encounter in any typical day. All of these doubts and questions, these commitments and obligations, have a sound basis and are well meaning at their core. And all of us struggle to find the right mix of priorities within our lives each and every day, myself included. The objection we often raise is: "I just don't have the time to invest in someone else's life right now, but maybe when X happens, or after Y is finished." Insert your own scheduling conflicts, agendas, or what have you into the blanks.

What we are asking is not that anyone needs to replicate Jesus's life, but that we be willing to disciple in the manner that He discipled His own followers. Jesus modeled this *in spite* of culture and *in spite* of the fact that most everyone following Him wanted a piece of His time. Of course He was unique in that He was the Son of God, and yet do we not have the same Spirit within us? The Holy Spirit is prompting us toward relationship. With God and with others. Always.

Again I will say, when Jesus said, "Do as I have done," in any of His teachings, He was not looking for perfection. What He was most concerned with was the effort, welling up from the heart of His followers, through the prompting of the Holy Spirit. The amount of people was never the issue. The time involved was never the issue. To Jesus, it is the right-standing of the heart, and the willingness to become intentional, even if that intentionality of relationship is with one person for one hour a week.

The question shouldn't be, "How can I possibly do this?" The question should be, "What can I do in the time that I've already been given?" And the second one should be like it: "Who can I intentionally become more involved with who's already within my sphere of influence?"

Maybe we should return to the methods of Jesus, knowing that His message was divinely inspired, but also trusting that His *methods* were divinely inspired as well. He walked with the men He discipled. He talked with them. He ate with them. He asked them questions. He listened to them. He prayed with them. He fished with them. He sent them out. He checked in with them when they returned. He corrected them when they made mistakes.

And, most importantly, He loved them the entire time.

Whatever it happened to take, within the time He was with these men, He used it to invest into their lives with the message and purpose that He had been given. This is the same message and purpose that the apostles passed on to the first church and so on and so on, all the way down to us today.

This model of intentional, relational discipleship is something that we can do, and are being asked to do, even today. Within our time constraints. Within our cultures and traditions. Honoring those things, yes, but investing the time within those traditions in order to create deep, abiding relationships, ultimately creating disciples and a discipleship model that can be replicated in order to create disciples who create more disciples who create...you get the idea.

The Model of Today's Church

Overall, what we're talking about here is a model used by many of today's churches around the world—a model either begun by well-meaning men and women, or patterned after the examples of well-meaning missionaries from many countries over the past decades. A model that has been somewhat shifted so that it no longer resembles the model that Jesus personified with His disciples. The problem with the model used by many of today's churches is twofold. First, it is based on a flawed template, a template we've been detailing over the last several chapters. The second is that this well-intended church model is both unrealistic and unsustainable.

Here's what I mean. In a typical church today, the senior pastor, who some see as the "star player" or the "paid player" of the church "team," sees his job as shepherding and protecting his sheep. In his mind, he must protect his sheep from the world, because the "world" is bad and, of course, God is good. The two ways he will often do this is to deliver a Sunday message where he will offer up "the truth," and the other way is that if any of the sheep get injured or sick, he will help them through this difficult time; he will visit them in the hospital, he will counsel them, he will pray for (and with) them, and so on. If possible, there may be a few people who can help the senior pastor in this regard, but overall, this is what the pastor is paid to do, at least in the eyes of those who pay his salary (i.e., the congregation).

Within this self-appointed role, the pastor can effectively shepherd forty, fifty, maybe up to one hundred people. But, past that point, he begins to become less and less effective at each appointed task. Soon, he becomes exhausted. He starts to get overburdened. Feelings of failure begin to creep in. His health begins to falter as fatigue and stress take their toll.

Within the church, once we cross this line where the pastor begins to become less effective, the fruits of spiritual growth begin to stagnate and wither on the vine. The congregation starts to feel neglected, a burden, a bother, not unlike the child of a workaholic parent feeling as though the parent doesn't even love them anymore, even though that parent may have the best of intentions in "providing" for his or her family.

The pastor loves his congregation very much, and they love him. But the relationship between the two, and between individual members, becomes distant and strained nonetheless, and eventually dries up and dies.

The *Biblical* Model of Church

> *So Christ himself gave the apostles, the prophets, the evangelists, the pastors and teachers, to equip his people for works of service, so that the body of Christ may be built up until we all reach unity in the faith and in the knowledge of the Son of God and become mature, attaining to the whole measure of the fullness of Christ.*
>
> *Then we will no longer be infants, tossed back and forth by the waves, and blown*

here and there by every wind of teaching and by the cunning and craftiness of people in their deceitful scheming. Instead, speaking the truth in love, we will grow to become in every respect the mature body of him who is the head, that is, Christ. From him the whole body, joined and held together by every supporting ligament, grows and builds itself up in love, as each part does its work. — Ephesians 4:11–16, NIV

Here, along with all the passages we see on making disciples, and going into the world, we see that God gave *all* of these people to equip the saints for the work of the ministry. This model is the exact opposite of the model of today's typical church. Here we see that a pastor is given a vast palette of people to draw from. Within this framework, a pastor can invest in a select few of his closest associates, equipping and discipling them for "works of service." In turn, each of these disciples, invested in by one man, can equip and disciple others, radiating out like ripples in a pond, exponentially, rather than down a singular line, one at a time, like dominoes.

In the Biblical model—Jesus's model—the disciples, the congregation, and each church member are being equipped and released to "go and make disciples," not leaving this commission solely to the work of one pastor. Not all of us are called to be apostles, prophets, evangelists, pastors, or teachers. But each of us is called to be His people—God's people—equipped and released for works of service so that the whole body of Christ may be built up, unified, and mature, "attaining to the whole measure of the fullness of Christ."

This is not a Dave Campbell concept, a Kent Roberts concept, or a Real Life Ministries concept. This is *God's* concept. That's why it works. That's why it *will* work.

Regardless of time and tradition constraints, it works. Every. Single. Time.

This vast field of disciples and this army, rather than one, lone man, can then be unleashed into the world, "so that the body of Christ may be built up until we all reach unity in the faith and in the knowledge of the Son of God."

In other words, disciples unleashed!

> *"Therefore go and make disciples of all nations, baptizing them in the name of the Father and of the Son and of the Holy Spirit, and teaching them to obey everything I have commanded you. And surely I am with you always, to the very end of the age."* — Matthew 28:19–20, NIV

This model only works when we, His followers, invest in one, two, or only a few people at a time rather than hundreds, or even forty or fifty. Only within this small circle of our closest associates can we model this intentional discipleship, investing in only a few, who can then invest in a few, and on and on. The faces within the "few" may change over time, as disciples are raised up and "unleashed," but the key lies in the concentration of effort within only that select few at any one time.

Today's model of church would rather keep our congregations safe and secure in a box, to be protected and fed by the pastor, rather than helping them grow up into spiritual warriors, unleashing them into the enemy territory (spiritually speaking) that is our world today.

So What Makes the Difference? What Is All This Life-On-Life Stuff?

What the typical model of "church" and "relationship" has devolved into today is more akin to disciple-making through imparting information. In other words, if I tell you something, Biblically speaking, that is "true," I am discipling you.

Doing life together means that we know each other well enough that we can speak truth to one another, regardless of time, regardless of distance, and regardless of circumstance. This truth does not have to be doctrinal, though it will be Biblically based. This truth can be social, it can be relational, and it can be speaking into a struggle, an addiction, or a conflict. It can be any number of things, spoken honestly and, at times, courageously, into the life of another person.

Courage flows both ways though in this type of relationship. Of course there is the courage to say what may *need* to be said rather than what the other person *wants* to hear. But there is also courage within the heart of the listener in order to be receptive and responsive to what may be said in love and honesty. We may not agree with what is being said, but we also don't automatically lash out in anger or defensiveness simply because the person is speaking to us what may be difficult for us to hear.

There is a certain level of superficiality that permeates a good amount of today's church culture. I may see you in church and know you well enough to say, "Hi," or maybe ask, "How's it going?" You would likely respond, "Fine, praise God!" Then our families might sit with one another during the service, and afterward we would go our separate ways.

And we would call this interaction "friendship," maybe even "relationship."

Turning that into a life-on-life relationship, or for us to "do life" together, means that you and I know each other to the point where we're actually going to be honest with each other about how we're doing in our marriage, how we're doing with our kids, how I'm doing in my walk with the Lord, how my prayer life is going, and what am I struggling with. We're going be honest enough to be able to talk with each other about these issues and help each other through them by pointing each other to Biblical truth and holding each other accountable.

It means when my wife is physically sick or mentally down, your family might bring us a meal.

It means when your child is injured and in the hospital, we come and visit you there, consoling and praying, offering help or whatever it takes to usher you through this crisis.

It also means having fun together, going to dinner, or going to ball games or to a concert, whatever our shared, common interests may be.

It means that if you have to call me at 3 a.m. because of something that has come up, you can do that. In fact, I would want and expect you to do that.

In other words, this deeper form of relationship means helping each other through this journey called "life," and focusing on how we are doing at being disciples and how we are doing at making disciples.

A couple questions may still be springing to mind about the time and relational factor of this type of intentional relationship. For instance, does this mean we have to go out and, with purpose and intention, find our "one" to invest time in with this type of relationship?

Sometimes, but more often than not, no. More than likely you already have certain names and faces coming to mind of people you already spend time with, and in whom this type of relational discipleship would be the next logical step in your relationship.

Does this mean that Jesus asks us to dive into this deeper, more intentional form of connection with every person we know?

Again, of course not. But we should be asking God for the guidance to help us in finding such a person or such a family, one that would be open to and interested in this form of relationship. Then we would need to follow up on the Holy Spirit's prompting when the opportunity does present itself. Because it will.

Maybe this prompting leads you no further than your immediate family: your spouse and your kids. You need to know that that is not only okay, it's expected. Discipleship starts in the home! You already have a sphere of relationships that can be furthered with a little intentional focus on Biblical discipleship. For instance, I have a relationship with my wife. How can I become more intentional within this relationship? Two ways come to mind.

First, I should be impacting her in that my growing as a follower of Christ needs to be evident to her, and the changes that Jesus is making in me should have a positive correlation to our relationship. For although Ephesians 5:22 says, "Wives, submit yourselves to your own husbands...," this submission would be done a lot more willingly if the husbands were to heed what Paul followed with in Ephesians 5:25–26: "Husbands, love your wives, just as Christ loved the church and gave himself up for her to make her holy, cleansing her by the washing with water through the word."

I may have once been a bit of an authoritative dictator around our house, but as I have committed to being a follower of Christ, God has helped me to become more sacrificial in our relationship, setting my wife apart and meeting her needs before my own, giving myself up for her to make her holy, and also reading Scripture together and speaking Biblical truth into her life through both words and actions, cleansing her by the washing with water through the Word.

Second, as a natural extension of this intentional relationship, I should also be open to discipleship *from* my wife. She is the one who can hold me most accountable. She should be the one to speak truth into my life as no one else can, or at times should. She should also be my greatest source of encouragement and strength.

Relationship is a two-way street, as are honesty and courage. Only when we can safely and securely travel both ways on these streets can we then give and receive what Paul in Ephesians writes as "speaking the truth in love."

And speaking of the role of wives and other women in this model of relational discipleship brings up another key point. Internationally, I think we find that this is a really important distinction to make, in that pastors and leaders need to recognize that women are just as capable, and it seems more *willing* than men, to be disciples who can make disciples.

Our mission teams are working in dozens of countries and cultures around the world, and we are seeing spiritual fruit in each and every one of those countries and cultures by following Jesus's model of relationship. The key lies in distilling the Biblical principle and model and applying that within your own culture, to not get hung up on the peripheral things that distinguish cultural acceptance. For instance, if within a certain culture it is necessary to remove one's shoes before entering a room and to sit a certain way, then that is what you do. That's okay. We don't have to sit in a circle or hold hands when we pray. These are not Biblically-based principles. We don't have to sit in a large room with a stage and a microphone and have the Word of God spoken *at* us. We can, and we are expected to, discuss the Word within our own spheres of influence among family, friends, and work associates, to discuss its applications in our lives and in our families, to wrestle with Biblical truth, and to hold each other accountable, in love and in support.

Pastor Pablo in the Heart of Ecuador

Loja, Ecuador, is a hotbed of conservative Catholicism. As far as Evangelical Christianity, it has one of the lowest percentages of population in all of South America. Cisne, a town nearby, has a very famous and ornate chapel to the Virgin of Cisne. As far as the surrounding natural beauty, the area around Loja is unsurpassed; it is lush, green and fertile, which makes it understandable that the region is heavily agricultural. In the midst of this environment, and this culture, there is maybe a small, single-digit percentage of those who would call themselves Christians.

Because of the strength of the conservative Catholicism permeating the region, and the relatively low populace of Evangelicals, there has been what I would call a "bunker mentality" within the Christian community in that the overriding feeling is one of, "I am a Christian, I am a believer, but I'm not going to talk about that outside the walls of our church." These relatively few people feel protected within their churches, but outside, though they are believers, they are hesitant to proclaim their faith and pretty much try to be just a "good person."

Thus was the mindset and overriding cultural chasm we encountered as we tried to speak about the concept of Biblical discipleship—of doing life together, of transparency and honesty, of sharing each other's burdens. What a foreign concept it was to them! Repellent, even! Though there were a few relative similarities between the two religions, there still existed a level of persecution within the community of Loja toward the Evangelical believers.

In Chapter 3 I related the story of a conference that was held down in Ecuador, where we were attempting to discuss Jesus's model of relational discipleship in a small-group setting.

And, It Works in All Cultures...Even Yours

Within the group of pastors gathered there, the discussion came around to the point of talking about being vulnerable—not just with each other, but within their congregations and within their communities. I remember the furrowed brows and the muttered comments to one another. They had shared the relative comfort and safety of talking with each other within this group, at this time, and it had impacted them greatly, but it also hit them they would have to recreate this same culture of transparency within their own churches and communities. That's when they spent the next forty-five minutes—with little direction from me—on the questions of, *Can we do this? Is the cost worth it? Do I have the time? If I do this, will I lose my job? Will people turn against me, finding me unfit to be a pastor?*

They knew that if they chose this path within their own churches and spheres of relationship, people could use such vulnerability, and such admissions of weakness or fault, and likely hurt them, whether emotionally, physically, or monetarily. Something like what we were asking them to do, moreover what *Jesus* was asking of them, could very well cost them their jobs, their reputations, or their lives.

Eventually, by consensus, the group came to a decision. After weighing the risks, weighing what God was asking, both the benefits and the danger, the group felt overwhelmingly moved to continue modeling what they had come to learn from our time together. They chose to pass on to their families, and their churches, the fruit of what they were seeing among themselves, in spite of any risk involved.

This was the culture of Ecuador, of Loja, and even in the midst of this culture, Pastor Pablo Celi was one of the pastors who made this bold decision.

Pablo has a very dynamic, growing ministry of multiple churches in the Loja area. He is following up on this Biblical church model that we discussed based on Ephesians 4:11–16, equipping all of his people for works of service so that the body of Christ may be built up.

Together, they are making disciples who are making disciples. He and his congregation are stepping boldly out of their "bunker" mentality, proclaiming their faith, talking with people, answering questions, and meeting needs, no matter the person or the circumstance. And, despite the odds and small percentages, what they thought would never work in that culture *is* working, and the community has been much more receptive to their message and methods than even they thought possible.

People are hungry for real relationship. They are hungry to know about Jesus.

The overriding truth is that this is how God designed us. We are designed for real relationship—both with each other and with God.

And this is what I find just as interesting and why I even bring up Pastor Pablo...

When we first came to Loja, Pablo was one of the most successful Evangelical pastors of the region. He is the president of the Pastoral Association of Evangelical Pastors. He very easily could have said, "What I've got is working. We don't need what you have at all. Who are you to come in and try to teach us anything? You don't live here, and you don't know what goes on."

Instead he was very humble and eager to learn. After we spent a couple of days with him, he announced to his whole church that though they had been successful and they were growing, "we have been sent these people to give us a part of God's plan that we did not have."

All we added was the concept of real relationship, of doing life together and investing in one another's needs, and strengths, and weaknesses. Continually what we were told by the people was that "you are showing us how to love each other."

What we showed them was nothing more than what Jesus showed to His disciples, what the people showed to each other in the early churches of Acts 2 and 4, and what we are called to show each other today. And it will work in every culture. It already has. Not because of any designs of man, but because this was the way our Creator designed us all along—for relationship, for connection, for discipleship.

So let's get down to the basics of what this intentional, relational discipleship is all about...

And, It Works in All Cultures...Even Yours

Bible verses to consider

Ephesians 4:11-16   Matthew 28:18-20

2 Timothy 2:2

Study questions for further discussion

*Why does Jesus's model of relationship, discipleship, and church work in every single culture?

*How can you help your church community overcome some of the cultural obstacles that may be standing in the way of true, biblical relationship?

*How would you go about implementing life-on-life discipleship with someone? (Be specific)

Chapter 10
Getting Down to the Basics

Boiling it down to basics begins with understanding the target, knowing that it starts with being a disciple, making disciples, and radiating out from our own understanding, into our family, into the church, into the community, and into the world.

So, how do we do this? Let's return to Ephesians for a moment.

> *So Christ himself gave the apostles, the prophets, the evangelists, the pastors and teachers, to equip his people for works of service, so that the body of Christ may be built up until we all reach unity in the faith and in the knowledge of the Son of God and become mature, attaining to the whole measure of the fullness of Christ.*
>
> *Then we will no longer be infants, tossed back and forth by the waves, and blown here and there by every wind of teaching and by the cunning and craftiness of people in their deceitful scheming. Instead, speaking the truth in love, we will grow to become in every respect the mature body of him who is the head, that is, Christ. From him the whole body, joined and held together by every supporting ligament, grows and builds itself up in love, as each part does its work.* — Ephesians 4:11–16, NIV

Whether you are an apostle, a pastor, a teacher, or "just" a church member (see Thom S. Rainer's book, *I Am a Church Member*), you are a disciple. This is the job that God has given us all, to "equip his people for works of service, so that the body of Christ may be built up."

The whole body of Christ is then geared to accomplish the works we were meant to accomplish.

> *For we are God's handiwork, created in Christ Jesus to do good works, which God prepared in advance for us to do.* — Ephesians 2:10, NIV

The way to accomplish this isn't merely through acquiring knowledge; it is through growing in relationship with God and others, and learning through love how to walk that out.

An excellent example of the difference between growing in knowledge and growing in relationship and love can be found in 1 Corinthians chapters 12 and 13. Chapter 12, starting in verse 12, is all about the unity and diversity of the body of Christ and how we are all called to play our part in growing and maturing the body, each with our own unique part to play. The chapter ends with this verse: "And yet I will show you the most excellent way" (NIV).

I don't know if you know this, my friends, but within Paul's original letters (in fact, in all Gospels, Epistles, and books of the Bible), there were no chapters or verse numbers. So, chapter 13 is a natural extension of Paul's thoughts in chapter 12, with the transitional sentence being, "And yet I will show you the most excellent way." In other words, "Here's how you should go about doing what we just talked about—being a vital member of the body of Christ, and helping all to reach unity and maturity."

Many of us know chapter 13 of 1 Corinthians as the "love chapter"—love is patient, love is kind, if I speak with the tongues of angels and have not love I am only a resounding gong, and so on.

So, according to the Apostle Paul, how does one build up the body of Christ, reaching unity and maturity and the "fullness of Christ"?

Through love.

And how do we show deep and abiding love for one another?

Through relationship.

It's almost as if God planned it this way all along.

(Yes, that was sarcasm.)

Paul echoes these same ideals with his letter to the Ephesians. We are called to "equip [God's] people for works of service, so that the body of Christ may be built up until we all reach unity in the faith and in the knowledge of the Son of God and become mature, attaining to the whole measure of the fullness of Christ... Speaking the truth in love, we will grow to become in every respect the mature body of him who is the head, that is, Christ...build[ing] itself up in love as each part does its work."

As we wrote earlier in this book, Jesus was asked what the greatest commandment was, and He gave His answer in two parts: "'Love the Lord your God with all your heart and with all your soul and with all your mind.' This is the first and greatest commandment. And the second is like it: 'Love your neighbor as yourself.'" He gave them two answers even though they only asked for one, because the two answers He gave were so inseparably intertwined.

So, what are the "basics" that we're boiling it all down to?

Love

He is the one we proclaim, admonishing and teaching everyone with all wisdom, so that we may present everyone fully mature in Christ. — Colossians 1:28, NIV

Love.

Because "all the laws and the prophets hang on these two commandments," and they hang on this one overriding principle.

Relationship.

Love.

Only when we begin abiding by these most important commandments can we then dig into all of the "one another's" of the Bible, how we can bear one another's burdens, how we forgive one another, how we are patient with one another. This is how relationships, and the foundations of discipleship, are incubated and grown, following these two basic principles: loving God and loving others. Those who are believers but are not yet spiritually mature can still be *self*-centered; their focus, their intentions, and even their relationships revolve around "self" and what benefit these things can be to "them." As God transforms us, we grow to become more and more *God*-centered and *other*-centered as well—our focus becomes more about what we can do for God and for others, and our relationships become more intentional to that end.

> *Don't be selfish; don't try to impress others. Be humble, thinking of others as better than yourselves. Don't look out only for your own interests, but take an interest in others, too.*
> *You must have the same attitude that Christ Jesus had.*
> *Though he was God,*
> *he did not think of equality with God as something to cling to.*
> *Instead, he gave up his divine privileges;*
> *he took the humble position of a slave and was born as a human being.*
> *When he appeared in human form, he humbled himself in obedience to God*
> *and died a criminal's death on a cross.* — Philippians 2:3–8, NLT

These principles are clearly what we see in the church of the early chapters of Acts.

Unfortunately, the modern church today has taken Jesus's Great Commission to "go and make disciples of all nations...teaching them to obey everything I have commanded you" and morphed it into "Here's a twelve-week course on Biblical truth and once you're done with that, then you're a disciple." This is the "informational dump" investment of time that we've talked about in the previous chapter. This is what people (well-meaning pastors and churchgoers) have come to expect whenever we begin a discussion on the Biblical model of relational discipleship.

It should be obvious by now that this mentality of "information dump" isn't what Jesus meant, by any stretch. The apostles had just spent three years with Jesus as He lived with them, ate with them, discipled them, and taught them. Therefore, it stands to reason that when He says, "Teach them to obey everything I have commanded you," they would know not only *what* He was asking them to teach, but *how* He was asking them to teach it—by the investment of time, by intentional relationship, by devoting ourselves to teaching, yes, but by meeting each other's needs, by meeting together, and by being of one heart and mind.

Pastor Ronald

Kizito Ronald, or "Pastor Ronald," as we call him, is the lead pastor for Living Springs Church of Christ in Fort Portal, Uganda, a city of roughly 45,000 to 50,000 people 200 miles west of the capital city of Kampala. He holds services within his church for well over 1,000 people at a time, and his facilities include an orphanage and a recently completed medical clinic. He also hosts a weekly radio show that has grown his church attendance by leaps and bounds since he first started less than two years ago.

When I first met Ronald, and not unlike many of the pastors we've talked about throughout this book so far, he was one who fit the mold of a very structured and authoritarian style of leadership and preaching. He taught the Word, and the congregation listened and took away whatever they could from the day's message. Again, this was through no fault of his own; like so many of the other pastors we've discussed, this was the only way Ronald knew how to shepherd his flock and to preach. This was the only model that he had ever been shown.

The first time we met was in Burundi, a small, neighboring country to the south of Uganda and a twenty-two-hour bus ride for Ronald from his home church in Fort Portal. We were meeting with a group of pastors from several neighboring countries about relational discipleship, and Ronald in particular was a sponge for all we were talking about; he soaked it all in, embracing it eagerly.

The next year he was able to make the trip to Real Life Ministries and attend one of our DiscipleShift courses (then called Immersion). One of our opening "ice breaker" exercises is a learning activity called Pipeline, in which they were moving a small ball a certain distance along a series of handheld channels. How a team accomplishes the objective they set is totally up to them. The main challenge to overcome is that the participant with the ball cannot move their feet—passing the ball using their channels is fine, just don't shuffle your feet in the process.

Ronald's group included about twelve people, and Ronald became a sort of self-appointed leader. Back then, he was a very strict "letter of the law" kind of guy, both in his preaching and in his life. One fellow group member, a man from Ethiopia, kept moving his feet. Ronald would remind him, and rebuke him, but it didn't seem to help. Time after time, the man just kept moving his feet whenever he had the ball.

After two or three rebukes, and the ball going back to the beginning with each misstep, the next time the man moved his feet Ronald took his own wooden tray and whacked him on the back of his legs saying, "Don't move or I will cane you again!"

Needless to say, when we gathered together as a group for the debriefing following the exercise, there was plenty of baggage to unpack!

We have a couple, Paul and Stefanie Byrns, from our missions team that travels to Fort Portal once or twice a year. We have also had the opportunity to travel to a few of the surrounding countries including Burundi and the Congo, where we've been able to meet up with Ronald, spend some time with him, and check into his progress of discipleship and church growth as well as his relationships with his family and his staff.

I have been amazed to watch the growth in Ronald over this time, particularly in his desire to get down to the basics of love and relationship, as he has spent time with both our staff and with his own. We've done nothing more in his presence than live out what intentional relationship looks like. When they travel to Uganda, Paul and Stefanie, as well as the rest of our

Getting Down to the Basics

staff, meet with Ronald and his wife, along with some of his staff and their spouses from time to time, and do nothing more at times than enjoy good conversation, good food, and good fellowship—"breaking bread in their homes and eating together with glad and sincere hearts, praising God and enjoying the favor of all the people" (Acts 2:46, paraphrased). Of course there is purpose in our Missions trips to share the Gospel, and to help where help is needed. But there are also times when we can be intentional in our *un*-intentionality, because fellowship *can* be discipleship and discipleship, at the best of times, looks an awful lot like fellowship.

In the ensuing years after the Pipeline incident, Ronald has continued to be a sponge in his desire to grow as a disciple, and as one who disciples others. From the time spent with our staff and missions team, he has begun to learn what intentional relationships look like, seeing lived out what discipleship means within families and friends, and seeing the fruits of Jesus's model and methods as he passes them on to his own church and community.

It's been a tough journey for Ronald. Uganda is one of those cultures where Christianity has come into an almost tribal tradition. The pastor at times can easily assume a role of both "pastor" and "chief," which would have been an easy model for Ronald to slip into, as his own family has a history of tribal leaders and witch doctors among their ancestry. Honestly, it was a road we saw Ronald venturing down when we first met him (as evidenced by the Pipeline encounter). Still, the change we have seen within him has been dramatic.

I was over in Uganda with Ronald a little less than a year ago and we were talking with some of the key leaders of his church, and we asked them pointedly, "What is the thing that you see that attracts you to the leadership of Ronald?"

The answer was unanimous. It was the love that Ronald genuinely showed to each and every one of them, and to the congregation as a whole.

The willingness with which we saw Ronald embrace Jesus's model of relational discipleship, the transparency and the honesty, the eagerness to pass on this example of Biblical discipleship—to his family and to his staff—and the receptivity with which this love and intentionality was embraced by his closest advisors, laid any concerns or questioning we had to rest with this one resounding answer from the staff themselves.

When we heard Ronald's people say that, we knew Ronald got it!

The path to being a real disciple is love. This is the simplest path. Not to say that it is an *easy* path, but it is often the most direct way. It is God's way, the way of making true disciples of Jesus who can then make disciples who make disciples, and so on.

It is nothing more or less than what we said in the first few chapters of this book: the bringing together of the Greatest Commandment and the Great Commission—to be love, to have love, and to show love.

> *As the Father has loved me, so have I loved you. Now remain in my love. If you keep my commands, you will remain in my love, just as I have kept my Father's commands and remain in his love. I have told you this so that my joy may be in you and that your joy may be complete. My command is this: Love each other as I have loved you. Greater love has no one than this: to lay down one's life for one's friends.* — John 15:9–13, NIV

Now it's time to apply what we've discovered throughout this book. It's time for the rubber to meet the road. It's time to unleash some disciples!

Bible verses to consider

Ephesians 4:11-16   Colossians 1:28

Ephesians 2:10   John 15:9-13

1 Cor. 12:12-13:13

Study questions for further discussion

*What have you learned so far about Biblical love and Biblical relationships? How does that differ from what you thought before reading this book?

*What did Ronald's story teach you about yourself?

*How will you apply some of the things you may have learned in your life?

*Do you have someone in your life—a friend, co-worker, or family member perhaps—with whom you can be completely open, authentic, transparent and vulnerable? (Someone who is spiritually mature)

Disciples Unleashed

Chapter 11
Where the Rubber Meets the Road

Now we know the truth.
Now we see the picture.
Now we know where we should go.

We've read stories of pastors who have done the best that they can with what they have been shown, and yet when we see "the best we know to do" contrasted with the Biblical model, we see that Jesus's model and method really are what strike a chord within people's hearts. We inherently know it is the right and perfect model, because we have been inherently designed to crave this type of relationship—both with God and with others.

The question now becomes, are we going to pursue the model that Jesus has shown us? How we choose to answer this question hinges on the dichotomy that, as we have also seen, following this model is both very simple and very difficult at the same time.

It's easy to put on a good Sunday service with a great message and a dynamic worship, and draw in 500 or more people as we do.

It becomes a little more difficult to become involved in people's lives, in relationships that can become messy and tense, where real people are involved in real life struggles. Where we're asked to get our hands dirty and walk with these people through their "stuff." Where we need to be okay with those same people wading into our "stuff." Where the outcome may not always be as easy and satisfying as a Hallmark movie, only knowing that having someone meet us where we are is a relief in itself.

As we've seen, we are not called to invest in a ton of people, spreading ourselves so thin that our own relationships, jobs, and health begin to suffer. The key is to begin where you are—in your family, with your friends, with your closest associates—to reach out in relationship, to pour into their lives, and then, by example and instruction, to have them pour into the lives of those within their own closest spheres. In other words, become a disciple who makes disciples who make disciples.

As we've also seen, this method of relational discipleship takes time. It takes effort. It takes intentionality. By the world's standards, those of us who choose to participate in Jesus's model could easily be seen as failures—not racking up the "big numbers," not having the flash and excitement of showmanship and staging and lighting, filling the brain with visual eye-candy but leaving the heart and soul empty and starving. Instead we choose to grow the way Jesus and the early church did, by relationship, by familiarity, by caring and sharing, and by love.

Dave's Story

Sometimes the answer (and method) we come to is a hybrid of the two—the world's model *and* Jesus's model. This is what happened to me, Dave.

I grew up learning to read by my dad teaching me to read the Bible. And, though I learned many Biblical truths at an early age, my family didn't put much stock in "church," which my family equated to organized religion and not in a good way. In fact, I didn't have much of a church connection at all until much later in life, and I didn't come to know an abiding relationship with the Lord and His church family until I was almost forty.

When I finally did establish this church connection, I came up through the ranks of ministry like many others who choose this career—beginning as a youth pastor, then an associate pastor, before the Lord led me out into the mission field. Once established in Missions, which I loved and had a particular affinity toward, my wife Janelle and I began a small, independent ministry, True Light Ministries, which joined together about twenty churches around the Pacific Northwest with about twenty churches down in Mexico. Within True Light, we would travel back and forth to our base in Tecate several times a year, working by ourselves or with groups on building projects, or in ministry, worship, and serving opportunities. We even had a church camp outside of Tecate, where groups could gather and meet year round.

This was all well and good, and our ministry saw a decent harvest of fruit, both in the States and in Mexico. Yet there was still something skewed in what I was modeling, in my ministry and in my family.

You see, when I did come to the Lord, I saw, like so many before me, what had always been modeled in the American church—a one-way message, an authoritarian style of leadership, and not a lot of investment into the lives and relationships of the congregational members. Something was missing, and at the time I had no idea what it could possibly be, or even that I knew this piece was missing.

It wasn't until a few years later when I was contacted by one of the pastors for Real Life Ministries—a young man I had known from when he had come to Mexico with one of the mission teams the church had sent—about sending a small team of RLM kids to Mexico for a Missions trip, that the scales covering my eyes began to slough away. Janelle and I were invited to take a two-day program on discipleship (then called Immersion, now DiscipleShift) and learn more of what the central focus of Real Life was all about. (This is not to say that discipleship is a Real Life Ministries idea, but discipleship is the central, unifying purpose of why RLM exists as a church.)

These two days changed our lives.

First of all, I asked myself how, through the time I'd spent in ministry, and the time Janelle and I had been attending church, we could miss all of this—Jesus's model; relational discipleship; the benefits of gathering together and sharing all we had, including our very lives. I knew that not only had my wife and I benefitted from this experience, but I had to pass this on to the churches we worked with down in Mexico.

Like so many pastors that come through DiscipleShift, I learned what I could of the concepts and immediately wanted to share them with my own network of pastors and associates. (Remember the fire hydrant/bucket/thimble metaphor from Chapter 7?)

After a year or more of doing this, all the pastors I talked to received it with great excitement. I was excited too, but little fruit was being produced in any of the churches where my narrow view of discipleship was being passed on.

Eventually, it came to me that, though I had been really good (especially in my own mind) at training these pastors out of my own, small bucketful of knowledge, I had done nothing toward actually living out the process within my own life. Of course, my reaction to this newfound revelation was, *I don't have time to live this out! I'm too busy training others how to do it to spend any time doing it myself!*

The answer I heard in response was a succinct, "You don't have a choice."

Where the Rubber Met the Road in My Life

How was I being a disciple? Who was I intentionally discipling?

Answering these questions cut down on a lot of my "training" of others, and brought that training home to my own heart, my own life, and my own family. This is where the rubber met the road within my own journey.

Too often, our temptation is to rush this newfound knowledge of Biblical, relational discipleship home to our staff and pastors, rushing to make small groups, appointing leaders for these networks of groups, and telling them what they need to do: "This is the model we're supposed to follow!" It doesn't work like that. Trust me, I know.

Where the rubber meets the road in all of our lives is the willingness of each of us to say that the center of this relational "target" we've been talking about throughout this book is *you*. It's *me*. Am I ready to be a disciple and to make disciples, starting within my own family and closest spheres of influence?

Being a disciple is as important as making a disciple. We can only reflect to others what God is truly doing in our own lives.

The modeling of discipleship begins with our own transformation, showing both ourselves and our closest relations how Jesus has changed us, opened us up, and transformed us into a true disciple of Christ, one who can now make disciples in the proper image of our Lord and Savior.

A Comparison and a Contrast: Philip and the Rich, Young Ruler

The rich, young ruler was a stringent follower of the law. He had the law down. Or at least he thought he did, until he asked Jesus the way to inherit eternal life.

> *Jesus said, "...If you want to enter life, keep the commandments."*
> *"Which ones?" he inquired.*
> *Jesus replied, "'You shall not murder, you shall not commit adultery, you shall not steal, you shall not give false testimony, honor your father and mother,' and 'love your neighbor as yourself.'"*
> *"All these I have kept," the young man said...* — Matthew 19:17b–20a, NIV

The man knew Jesus was a wise teacher, but like so many of us, he's looking for the "quick fix," the handbook, the bullet-point answer to that which will bring him fulfillment and eternal life, and so he presses Jesus:

> *"What do I still lack?"* — (verse 20b)

Jesus's answer was anything but a bullet-point list. It wasn't an answer at all (at least to the man's intended question). Instead, it was a life application and a heart change, wrapped in a "to do." But within this answer, Christ cuts to the core of what the man, and many of us, truly did lack:

> *Jesus answered, "If you want to be perfect, go, sell your possessions and give to the poor, and you will have treasure in heaven. Then come, follow me."* — (verse 21)

The subtle meanings behind this simple answer could fill another book, but the core of what Jesus was asking the man was not just to sell his possessions—it was to redirect his focus on what truly mattered to Jesus and to all of us: "*Then* come, follow me" (emphasis mine).

The man was holding on to a lot of "things": his wealth and his pride in adherence to the law, to mention just two. Jesus knew that what the man truly lacked was relationship—a relationship with Himself and likely a relationship with others.

This is where the rubber met the road for this young man. And, he chose poorly.

In contrast, Philip steps out in several opportunities, not always knowing the way or the outcome but being available, being compliant, and most importantly, being willing.

In other words, being a disciple.

In Acts chapter 6, Philip is one of the chosen seven to ensure the proper distribution of food among all of God's people, particularly the widows who were Hellenistic Jews. In Acts 8, following the persecution of the church and Stephen's martyrdom, Philip was one who traveled into Samaria...

> *...and proclaimed the Messiah there. When the crowds heard Philip and saw the signs he performed, they all paid close attention to what he said. For with shrieks, impure spirits came out of many, and many who were paralyzed or lame were healed. So there was great joy in that city.* — Acts 8:5–8, NIV

Then, no sooner had all of this been accomplished when the Lord called Philip to "go south to the road—the desert road—that goes down from Jerusalem to Gaza" (verse 26). No explanation, no bullet-point direction, just "go." And he does, which leads to his encounter with the Ethiopian eunuch, changing a man's life and an entire country's future and eternal destiny.

The Apostle Paul, another example of what a spectacular heart change can look like in the life of a disciple of Christ, describes his former life before meeting the risen Christ in this way in Philippians chapter 3:

> *"...circumcised on the eighth day, of the people of Israel, of the tribe of Benjamin, a Hebrew of Hebrews; in regard to the law, a Pharisee; as for zeal, persecuting the church; as for righteousness based on the law, faultless"* — (verses 5–6)

Then comes the life-changing "but":

> *"But whatever were gains to me I now consider loss for the sake of Christ. What is more, I consider everything a loss because of the surpassing worth of knowing Christ Jesus my Lord..."* — (verses 7–8)

We may not always know the direction the Lord calls us to go. We may not always know the outcome of our daily "encounters." (In fact, most times we likely won't.) The point is to be available anyway. To make mistakes, but to take the risks. To be willing, despite those times when the world calls us crazy or counterculture.

In other words: to be a disciple.

I believe getting back to the model of intentional, relational discipleship—Jesus's model—is a movement that God is creating and empowering, not just within one church, or one nation, but all around the world. Recently there was a conference held in the Philippines where over 10,000 pastors and associates gathered together to uncover a deeper understanding of what Jesus's model of discipleship looked like and how it applied to their lives and their cultures. Another conference, in Africa, that I was able to attend was also attended by pastors from over twenty-eight countries from around the nation and around the world. All of them have begun to ask the same question: "What is this discipleship that Jesus lived and modeled, what does it look like, and how do we do it?"

There is an awakening among pastors and leaders around the world that Biblical discipleship is the answer, regardless of the questions that are asked, the problems faced, or the cultures involved. Even if these questions have never fully formed in their minds, these men and women walk away from this discovery of relational discipleship convinced, on a heart and soul level, that this is Jesus's model and God's intention for His church and His people. This is the answer and the elusive key they have been searching for, both for church growth and spiritual growth, since congregants first began walking through their front doors.

What Are You Hoping to Learn Here?

So now we come full circle to the question I asked at the very introduction of this book: "What are you hoping to learn here?"

I pray that we have given you some tools and examples of how Jesus would have answered that question, using His model and God's inherent design for all of us.

We were designed for relationship, both to God and to others. This is the essence of the Greatest Commandment.

The entirety of the Gospels is the story of Jesus living out intentional relationship with His disciples—His closest three, His chosen twelve, and His hundreds of followers—even up to and after His death and resurrection. Jesus has asked us to do nothing less than what He has shown us in God's Word. This is the essence of the Great Commission.

We're not reinventing the wheel here. This model of relational discipleship is not some grand new plan or invention of Real Life Ministries.

This is God's plan.

This is Jesus's model.

If anything, we're merely stripping away the hundreds of years of "religiosity" that have permeated our doctrines and churches, laying bare the very essence of what God intended all along: to love God, and to love others, and to go and make disciples, teaching them all that Jesus has commanded and shown us.

Nothing more. Nothing less.

A Final Question

Let's take a look at our target analogy once again. What do we want to "aim" for?

Do we want a movement and multiplication of Jesus, His methods and message, spreading like wildfire across the world?

Do we want healthy, vibrant and exciting churches that follow in Jesus's model?

Do we want our brothers and sisters, as the church, bearing fruit for God's glory, stepping out boldly and planting new churches by the hundreds and even thousands?

Do we want to see the lost being saved, lives being transformed, and Satan on the run like the coward he is?

Then look again.

Picture our target in your mind's eye.

See the stand it sits on? This is the firm foundation of Biblical definitions that we spoke of in the beginning of this book. Definitions of disciple, of church, of Christian: *God's* definitions, not ours.

See the bull's-eye at the center? This is the crux of it all—"Be"-ing a real disciple of Jesus. This is where it all begins; by you, me, and all of us, being—by *His* definition—a true Christ follower and an authentic, active, difference-making disciple that makes disciples.

You. Me. All of us.

Disciple-makers.

As a new believer, I read passages such as Matthew 28:18-20 and thought, *there must be a mistake here. I can't make a disciple. That's God's job*! But now, wonder of wonders, I see His plan: He will do the heavy lifting; His is the transforming power; But He wants me—in fact, He tells me, and commands me—to "go and make disciples" for His glory. Therefore, if I truly am a disciple of Jesus, I *will* be a disciple-maker. And let's be clear here, anyone who calls himself a Christian, anyone who claims the name of Jesus Christ as Lord and Savior, *is* a disciple of Jesus.

And, this is one of the things a true disciple of Jesus does: Make more disciples.

But it all begins at the beginning. Focus on the bull's-eye. This must come first. Focus on the "Be", and the "make" will flow from there as will all the subsequent rings of our target, like ripples on a crystal clear pond. Miss the bull's-eye, however, and the rest will only fall apart, and both the target and the stand will crumble.

Starting right now, today, the arrow and the bow are in your hands dear reader.

Where do you choose to aim?

> *The harvest is great, but the workers are few. So pray to the Lord who is in charge of the harvest; ask him to send more workers into his fields.* — Luke 10:2, NLT

Our Prayer:

> Heavenly Father,
> You have said, "The harvest is great," and we know it is. We are asking today that You touch the hearts of all who read this book, to reach out to You and to each other, building bridges, building relationship, mending hearts, and repairing lives so that those who "work the fields" may feel strong and heartened by what they hear, from us, from each other, and most especially from You.
>
> Fill them with Your Spirit, Lord, and in doing so strengthen their relationships, strengthen their hearts, and build up your army of disciples unleashed, so that we may all reap a harvest beyond anything that we could possibly do on our own.
>
> All of this to Your glory and for Your kingdom.
> Amen.

Bible verses to consider

Matthew 4:19

Acts 8:5-8

Matthew 19:17-21

Luke 10:2

Study questions for further discussion

*What does Dave's story teach you about the difference between "knowing" and "being"?

*What might God be asking you to give up or change in your life today? In other words, what is keeping you from truly "being on mission" with Him?

*Pondering everything in this book, what are three key things (write them down please) God has shown you and how will you apply them in your life?

Disciples Unleashed

Made in the USA
Middletown, DE
13 June 2016